# Margaret Fuller's

## WOMAN IN THE NINETEENTH CENTURY

Recent Titles in
Contributions in Women's Studies

Marie Mitchell Olesen Urbanski

# Margaret Fuller's
## WOMAN IN THE NINETEENTH CENTURY

*A literary study of form and content,*
*of sources and influence*

Greenwood Press

*Contributions in Women's Studies,*
*Number 13*

Westport, Connecticut • London, England

*Library of Congress Cataloging in Publication Data*

Urbanski, Marie Mitchell Olesen.
  Margaret Fuller's Woman in the nineteenth century.

  (Contributions in women's studies; no. 13 ISSN 0147-104X)
  Bibliography:  p.
  Includes index.
  1. Ossoli, Sarah Margaret Fuller, marchesa d', 1810-1850.  Woman in the
nineteenth century.  2. Ossoli, Sarah Margaret Fuller, marchesa d', 1810-1850 —
Criticism and interpretation.  I. Title.
II. Series.
HQ1154.083U7     301.41'2'09034     79-7475
ISBN 0-313-21475-1

Library of Congress Catalog Card Number: 79-7475
ISBN: 0-313-21475-1
ISSN: 0147-104X

First published in 1980

Greenwood Press
A division of Congressional Information Service, Inc.
51 Riverside Avenue, Westport, Connecticut 06880

Printed in the United States of America

10 9 8 7 6 5 4 3 2 1

To my daughters, Jane Mercedes and Wanda Marie

"Always the soul says to us all, Cherish your best hopes as a faith, and abide by them in action."                                        *Margaret Fuller*

# Contents

# *Acknowledgments*

Two prominent writers who have written biographies of figures from the nineteenth century have been sources of encouragement and strength. Madeleine Stern, the Margaret Fuller biographer, deserves my gratitude for having read my work and made helpful suggestions for its improvement. To Howard N. Meyer, biographer of Thomas Wentworth Higginson and author of *The Amendment That Refused To Die*, acknowledgment is due for his early interest in my research.

American literature scholars owe a debt of gratitude to Joel Myerson for his achievement in compiling the Margaret Fuller bibliographies, but I would also like to express my appreciation to him for his analysis of my work and for his other scholarship in the field.

I am grateful to Harvard University's Houghton Library for permission to quote from material in its Margaret Fuller collection and to the New York Public Library for the use of its material, as well as to the Special Collections Section of the Margaret King Library of the University of Kentucky for the use of its rare books.

Recognition must be given to friends who have kept my morale up during periods of discouragement that seemed to follow a wave of enthusiasm and activity. My gratitude will always be due to these yea-sayers: Irene Haskett, Colleen Herrmann Demaris, Nancy MacKnight, and Beverly McCormick.

And paradoxically, I would like to thank those people who reacted negatively to my research. Their opposition made me realize how vital Margaret Fuller's thinking still is, and they challenged me to continue my work. Spurred on by the power of Margaret Fuller's ideas, I became aware of how much more Fuller research needed to be accomplished. In attempting such a task, I wish I could thank other women professors and mentors but their unfortunate absence from academia deprived me of the support I needed.

In my institution, the University of Maine, I would like to thank Joseph Loehr for some editorial assistance and Kathryn Belyea and Diane Kopec for handling the tedious job of typing with grace and intelligence.

Special acknowledgment is due to the fine editorial assistance given to me by the editorial board of Greenwood Press. The suggestions of Arlene Elder, Associate Professor of English, University of Cincinnati, made the final revision of my work much easier.

My greatest debt, however, I owe to my daughter, Wanda Urbánska. She is my most demanding critic; in her editorial assessment she is always uncompromising.

# Margaret Fuller's

## WOMAN IN THE NINETEENTH CENTURY

# Chapter 1 The denigration of Margaret Fuller as a writer

In 1903 Henry James said that "the unquestionably haunting Margaret-ghost" still lingered—over fifty years after Margaret Fuller's death—but he could not determine why.[1] In search of Fuller's memorial in Cambridge's Mount Auburn Cemetery, Susan B. Anthony attempted to recapture her spirit by finding the marker, but she was unable to locate it.[2]

Margaret Fuller remains as much of an enigma as she was in 1850 at the pinnacle of her career when she died so tragically off Fire Island. Few other people of the nineteenth century were as charismatic, or aroused as much admiration or as much anger, as did Fuller. The legend of her personality lingers to the detriment of appreciation by the intellectual establishment of her considerable achievements. She is the most important woman of the nineteenth century—its best literary critic, the first editor of the *Dial*, a nurse in an abortive Italian revolution (a precursor of both Florence Nightingale and Clara Barton), a woman who recognized the complicated emotional needs of women and men during the early stages of the repressive Victorian era, a foreign correspondent of the daily *New York Tribune*, and the author of numerous works, the most important of which is *Woman in the Nineteenth Century*, the intellectual foundation of the feminist movement.

Margaret Fuller was famous for both her magnetic personality and her intellectual accomplishments during her lifetime, but since her death, scholarly attention has focused on her personality. The paradoxes of Margaret Fuller were inexplicable to her contemporaries. She was a woman who was not considered physically pretty, yet she was captivating, and not humble but proud. Because of Fuller's unique behavior, attempts were made to explain it well before she died. But it was not until after her untimely death that the printed distortion of her personality began in the *Memoirs of Margaret Fuller Ossoli*, edited by Ralph Waldo Emerson, William Henry Channing, and James Freeman Clarke. This work became the literary canon that established Margaret Fuller as an arrogant "old maid," aggressive and ugly, the archetypal feminist whose need for attention was channeled into the feminist movement. In fact, this depiction of Fuller established the feminist archetype that remains today.

After delineating the distortion of her personality by key writers of the nineteenth century, it is the intention of this study to examine Fuller's *Woman in the Nineteenth Century* as a literary work.[3] Because her personality was so celebrated, scholars searching for concrete accomplishments to back up her reputation turned first to her literary rather than her social criticism because of its less inflammatory nature. It is for this reason that the first major American feminist work has not been given the attention it deserves, much less been recognized for the expression of genius that it is. Therefore, a corrective view of *Woman* as Fuller's germinal work is the ultimate purpose of this study.

Although Margaret Fuller's life has been the subject of numerous books, biographers have paid relatively little attention to *Woman*. This pattern was set in the *Memoirs of Margaret Fuller Ossoli*.[4] This first overall appraisal of Fuller as a woman and a writer was published in February 1852, less than two years after her death. The *Memoirs*, edited in some haste, set the pattern for subsequent biographers of focusing on Fuller's conversational brilliance and minimizing her writing ability. The personality picture is far from objective because of the editors' strong involvement with Fuller.

Perhaps the initial impetus behind publication of the *Memoirs* was to hush rumors of scandal surrounding Fuller's European sojourn. The editors attempted to explain Fuller's belated announcement

from Italy that she had a husband and a one-year-old child. Friends
and family in New England were still discussing her simultaneous
revelation of her secret marriage to the Marchese Giovanni Ossoli
and of the birth of their son, well over a year old, when they learned
of the tragic death of the family by drowning. All three were lost
from a ship that sank within sight of Fire Island, from which most
members of the crew and the captain's widow were able to save
themselves.

Interestingly enough, Emerson was reluctant to edit the *Memoirs*
because his "first decision was that Margaret had not been an
important enough figure to require a detailed memoir."[5] It was
Horace Greeley and William Henry Channing who persuaded him
to participate. Initially Samuel Ward also helped with the project,
although he later dropped out. The editors decided that the *Memoirs*
would consist of a two-volume collection of Fuller's key letters,
excerpts from her journal, eulogistic comments from friends and
associates, as well as those which each editor wrote. Unfortunately
the material was bowdlerized.

Most of the surviving Fuller manuscripts are in Harvard's Houghton Library.[6] When studying the remnants of her letters and journal, one feels frustrated at the careless mutilation by the editors of
the *Memoirs*, who not only destroyed and defaced original manuscripts but also rewrote Fuller's work, changing her writing style.
Scholars disagree as to the editors' motives. Perry Miller writes that
their standards of scholarship were of an earlier age before "profes-
sional canons" had emerged,[7] whereas Joseph Jay Deiss argues that
Emerson's scissors were "acting as censor's shears."[8] Yet the weight
of the evidence suggests that the excuses Miller made for the editors
were as biased as their original censorship. The extensive bowdleriz-
ing is important. Under the facade of reproduction of actual letters
and a journal, the editors rewrote history. What emerges, then, is
not Margaret Fuller (except in fragments) but the archetypal
feminist.

Although the *Memoirs* was edited by Emerson, Channing, and
Clarke, study of this work reveals that Emerson was the major
architect of the distortion of Fuller's reputation. Although probably
unconsciously, he established the Fuller canon—the feminist
archetype—which presents a portrait of an arrogant, aggressive

intellectual, who is not pretty. She is shown as an extremely emotional woman, not happy sexually, who is even interested in the occult.[9] Although not able to write, she can talk. Her personality cannot be ignored; she either repels or hypnotizes people. In the section of the work that Emerson edited are the remarks attributed to Fuller that have made her infamous: "I now know all the people worth knowing in America, and I find no intellect comparable to my own." Her complacency, Emerson said, astonished her friends. He reiterated her "overweening sense of power," her domination of her friends, her idealization of herself as a sovereign, and the presence of her "mountainous ME." Most people, Emerson wrote, were so repelled by their first encounter with Margaret that "they did not wish to be in the same room with her." He wrote of his first impressions: "Her extreme plainness,—a trick of incessantly opening and shutting her eyelids,—the nasal tone of her voice all repelled." Later he admitted that he had changed his mind and said he was wrong to stand in terror of a bluestocking—that she was a new Corinne who could make him laugh. Subsequently, he reiterated that she was "unattractive" and mentioned that he had expressed surprise to a friend that Margaret had received so many offers of marriage and homage from men in Europe.[10] And again with Yankee practicality, Emerson pointed out the difficulties that Fuller faced after her father's death—an orphan without beauty or money. In fact, much of his discussion in the *Memoirs* expresses his bewilderment as to the reasons for her appeal, and finally it hints guardedly that not only were the men in Europe attracted to Fuller, but so was he. Yet paradoxically he presented the woman he was attracted to as the feminist stereotype old maid—"Intellect I always have . . . shall the life never be sweet?" He quoted passages from her journal that indicated that the love she sought from men was frustrated.

Emerson's portrait even contains a germ of the feminist as lesbian that is so popular in the present day: "She had a feeling that she ought to have been a man, and said of herself, 'A man's ambition with a woman's heart is an evil lot.' "[11] At other times he noted "her burly masculine existence." "Her friendships, as a girl with girls, as a woman with women, were not unmingled with passion, and had passages of romantic sacrifice and of ecstatic fusion." Pointedly Emerson quoted: "It is so true that a woman may be in love with a woman, and a man with a man."[12] Thus Emerson's portrait contains some vestige of Fuller's understanding of the androgenous aspects of sexuality but also something of the feminist as frustrated or confused sexually. This image is sketched in Emerson's section, although toward the end of volume 2 an account is given (edited by both Emerson and Channing) of her marriage and motherhood, with little comment between letters.

Intrinsic to Emerson's Fuller canon is that she is irrational and interested in arcana, demonology, and mysticism. In her judgments she is subjective, susceptible to details, in art and nature, like the "victim of Lord Bacon's *idols of the cave*, or self-deceived."[13] As with other women, Emerson noted, Fuller's personal feeling colored all of her judgments. This is part of the reason why Emerson thought that Fuller could not write. And she herself acknowledged in her journals, to which Emerson had access, that her impatience with detail made writing difficult for her. She had a "long apprenticeship" with conversation in which she knew she shined and none with writing because her voice excited her, her pen never. But she "[will] write well yet," she vowed.[14] Unlike the inconsistent picture of her character that he presented, Emerson consistently argued that her "pen was a non-conductor." "In book or journal, she found a very imperfect expression of herself."[15] Emerson believed that her "only adequate channel" was "in her conversation," a judgment largely accepted to this day: Margaret Fuller was a great conversationalist, a personality whom people could not ignore, one that engendered either extravagant admiration or extreme dislike. The feminist archetype that Emerson created was one whose greatest power was not in her reason but in woman's traditional weapon—her tongue. Possessing mesmeric and occult power, Emerson's creation was as disturbing as a witch.

James Freeman Clarke's editorial assessment of Fuller was not unlike Emerson's: "Those who know Margaret only by her published writings know her least; her notes and letters contain more of her mind; but it was only in conversation that she was perfectly free and at home."[16] The Reverend Frederic Henry Hedge also echoed this view in his brief contribution to the *Memoirs*: "For some reason or other, she could never deliver herself in print as she did with her lips."[17]

But William Henry Channing was impressed when she confided in him that it was her "secret hope" that a woman could contribute to American literature. Instead of dogmatically denigrating her work, he quoted Horace Greeley's comments that Fuller's writing exhibited "intellectual wealth and force." Greeley at least noted that her writing style was characterized by "directness, terseness, and practicality" and "absolute truthfulness." She wrote "freshly, vigorously, but not always clearly," a fault he believed was due to the influence of the German literature she loved to read. What bothered him the most about her was her procrastination; he was impatient with her writing methods because she needed to wait for the "flow of inspiration" in order to write instead of performing like the "inveterate hack-horse of the daily press," who could meet deadlines.

Despite the Emersonian view that came to be generally accepted as to Fuller's "non-conducting pen," much of the *Memoirs* contains eulogy. If Fuller could not write, she could talk. If her first appearance were repulsive, those chosen to be initiated by Fuller would be converted. Hence, some of the remarks are not unlike those made at a wake, a time of hyperbole and fond anecdote. In a kind of hagiography, each editor recalled his first unforgettable impression of Fuller. Despite her reputation for biting satire and their initial apprehension, each one came to realize that beneath the proud exterior was a sensitive woman. Each man described his friendship with her in terms of a unique association.[18] Clarke wrote: "The intercourse was so intimate, and the friendship so personal, that it is like making a confession to the public of our most interior selves." Channing wrote that he could not convey "to readers my sense of the beauty of our relation, as it lies in the past with brightness falling on it from Margaret's risen spirit. It would be like printing a chapter of autobiography, to describe what is so grateful in memory, its influence upon one's self."[19]

As Emerson summed it up: "She drew her companions to surprising confessions." What seemed to have happened here is that she had a relationship at one time or another with the editors that could best be described as "soul mate"; at least she gave each man that impression. Greeley too followed the pattern of initial antagonism, which, like the others', gradually changed to admiration. He explained that Fuller had a large circle of admirers and that he was not one to burn incense on "any human shrine." Nevertheless, he conceded, he was inevitably drawn, "almost irresistibly, into the general current." He was careful to make it clear that it was at the suggestion of Mrs. Greeley, who had formed a "very high estimate" of Margaret's ability and a "warm attachment" for her, that he offered her a position in the literary department of the *New York Tribune*.[20] Part of the original offer contained the stipulation that Fuller could live at the Greeleys' home on the East River. In his contribution to the *Memoirs*, Greeley wrote in some detail about the love she felt for his son, which the child fully reciprocated.[21] The *Memoirs* was written by men who had recently learned of the scandal with Ossoli and, soon afterward, of the death of the family. Clarke had had an intense friendship with her and Channing a lesser one. Hence the *Memoirs* consists of emotional, and therefore subjective, appraisals of Fuller.

The *Memoirs* contains almost an anatomy of Fuller's baffling appeal. When Hedge, Channing, and Emerson conceded that she was not beautiful, they seemed to be unable to grasp the essence of her appeal. Perhaps Frederic Henry Hedge best expressed their descriptive dilemma:

> It was a face that fascinated without satisfying. Never seen in repose, never allowing a steady perusal of its features, it baffled every attempt to judge the character by physiognomical induction. You saw the evidence of a mighty force. . . .
>
> I said she had no pretensions to beauty. Yet she was not plain. She escaped the reproach of positive plainness, by her blond and abundant hair, by her excellent teeth, by her sparkling, dancing, busy eyes, which, though usually half closed from near-sightedness, shot piercing glances at those with whom she conversed, and, most of all, by the very peculiar and graceful carriage of her head and neck, which all who knew her will remember as the most characteristic trait in her personal appearance.[22]

And no one of them seemed more puzzled than Emerson.

Most biographers have observed the emotional involvement between Emerson and Fuller but stopped short of calling it love. The most frequently accepted interpretation is Carl F. Strauch's—that Fuller gradually "fell in love" with Emerson and that he repulsed her.[23] Another view is that the friendship was platonic. Biographers Madeleine Stern and Joseph Jay Deiss entertain the idea that Fuller's ambivalent love was reciprocated by Emerson. And careful analysis of Emerson's and Fuller's journals, as well as a study of their correspondence, makes this conclusion not impossible. It is important that the meticulous Emerson, who carefully preserved his letters, did not keep Fuller's letters written to him during the climactic period of their relationship in the fall of 1840. Emerson's journal entry for September 26, 1840, expresses the lovers' dilemma:

> You would have me love you. What shall I love? Your body? The supposition disgusts you. What you have thought and said? Well, whilst you were thinking and saying them, but not now. I see no possibility of loving anything but what now is, and is becoming; your courage, your enterprise, your budding affection, your opening thought, your prayer, I can love—but what else?[24]

After this journal entry, there is indication of some cooling of emotion. Emerson explained, "Our moods were very different," and he was "slow and cold. . . . A forlorn feeling was inevitable; a poor counting of thoughts, and a taking the census of virtues, was the unjust reception so much love found." Evidently, she did not find in him the emotional response she sought from her idealized mentor, for as she once expressed it, "I might not be able to be calm and chip marble with you any more."[25]

A few years later in New York, she fell in love with James Nathan, whereas Emerson still continued to be disturbed by her memory. Eight years later when he was in Paris, Emerson wrote to her in Italy, insisting that she return to the United States on the same ship with him. When she refused, he wrote again: "You will not wait but will come to London immediately and sail home with me." At this time, of course, he did not know that she was involved with Ossoli. He had even wanted to invite her to live with his family in Concord when she returned from Italy, but his wife, Lidian, objected to this plan.[26] When Emerson learned that Fuller had drowned, he confided to his journal: "I have lost in her my audience."[27] It was with a sense of grief at his loss, coupled with the jealous feeling that Ossoli had "taken her away"[28] from him, that he compiled the *Memoirs*.[29] The ambivalence of his position is unmistakable.

In his brief discussion of her published work, he did mention her translations and described her *Summer on the Lakes* as "an agreeable narrative." He discussed her editorship of the *Dial* in terms of her labor despite the poor compensation. Rather patronizingly he wrote: "She put so much heart into it."

Conspicuous by its omission in Emerson's section of the *Memoirs* is mention of *Woman in the Nineteenth Century*, an earlier version of which had been published in the *Dial* when he was editor. At that time, Emerson wrote to Fuller: "I think the piece very proper & noble, and itself quite an important fact in the history of Woman: good for its wit, excellent for its character—it wants an introduction: the subject is not quite distinctly & adequately propounded. It will teach us all to revise our habits of thinking on this head." He concluded by saying: "You will yourself write to this theme, whatever you write; you cannot otherwise."[30] He had even promised to write an introduction to the expanded version but then declined to do so.[31]

If Emerson made no direct reference in the *Memoirs* to *Woman*, he did to the issues that Fuller had raised in it:

Of the few events of her bright and blameless years, how many are private, and must remain so. In reciting the story of an affectionate and passionate woman, the voice lowers itself to a whisper, and becomes inaudible. A woman in our society finds her safety and happiness in exclusions and privacies. She congratulates herself when she is not called to the market, to the courts, to the polls, to the stage, or to the orchestra.

After developing this concept, he conceded that a revolution might be afoot. Then he explained that Margaret had no love of notoriety and that "willingly she was confined to the usual circles and methods of female talent."[32] This comment is absurd. All of Fuller's writing in one way or another expresses her frustration with the limitations that society placed on women. Emerson created this argument either to improve Fuller's image with the great majority of people, who were opposed to women's rights, or more likely, because it expressed his own sentimental but negative views on the subject rather than Fuller's.[33]

Clarke did not discuss *Woman* in the *Memoirs*, but Channing did mention it in rather vague terms. He quoted over three pages with the explanation that these extracts indicated her "spirit and aim." His choice of material to quote was mostly transcendental, and his comments about the book were in kind: "Thus, in communion with the serene loveliness of mother-earth, and inspired with memories of Isis and Ceres, of Minerva and Freia, and all the commanding forms beneath which earlier ages symbolized their sense of the Divine Spirit in woman, Margaret cherished visions of the future." Next, Channing turned to descriptions Fuller wrote of her visits with women prisoners at Sing-Sing. He did not make the obvious connection between the degraded prostitutes in prison and the application of Fuller's comments in *Woman* to their plight, except to say "Purgatory lies so nigh to Paradise."[34]

The discussion of Fuller's interest in social problems naturally led Channing to include Horace Greeley's comments about her work in New York. It was from Greeley that the only specific analysis of *Woman* came. Greeley wrote that he was first impressed by "The Great Lawsuit," the abbreviated title of her original essay published in the *Dial* that eventually matured into *Woman in the Nineteenth Century*: "I think this can hardly have failed to make a deep impression on the mind of every thoughtful reader, as the production of an original, vigorous, and earnest mind." Unlike other contributors to the *Memoirs*, Greeley delineated the social implications of Fuller's views. He complained that her ideas on female emancipation were inconsistent with the fact that she still expected to be treated with the deference accorded to a lady. He used to misquote mockingly her famous line—"Let them be sea-captains if they [*sic*] will!"—whenever he was performing the courtesies gentlemen accorded to ladies at that time. Other badinage between the two took place at the breakfast table when he used to lecture her on her dietetic habits, especially her reliance on tea and coffee.[35] Although Greeley did analyze *Woman* more cogently than the editors of the *Memoirs* did, the major thrust of his discussion focused on Fuller as a personality rather than as a writer and a thinker. The evidence suggests that the two-volume *Memoirs* was compiled in some haste by men whose emotions were too closely involved with Fuller as a person to render a dispassionate assessment of her work. Because Horace Greeley, William Henry Channing, and James Freeman Clarke were all influential and distinguished men of their time—and Ralph Waldo Emerson wore the mantle of a seer—subsequent biographers and critics have accepted their appraisal almost without question: Margaret Fuller was a great, egotistical personality rather than an original thinker or a brilliant writer.

The *Memoirs*, which has hitherto been the source book for Fuller study, should now be regarded as a judgmental nemesis. A readable account, the *Memoirs* was reviewed in many periodicals both in the United States and abroad, so its influence is enormous.[36]

The *Memoirs* remains as a valuable source of information about the transcendental movement, and it can be used as a tool for understanding Emerson.[37] In 1928, Helen Neill McMaster observed: "The part contributed by Emerson is valuable as a study in self-revelation, scarcely to be matched in his private Journals."[38] What McMaster said is a shrewd assessment. Emerson's portrait of Fuller in the *Memoirs* is in reality an unwitting self-revelation. He admitted that he did not like to laugh too much but that Fuller made him do so, "more than I liked." This statement reveals both his humorless personality and the fact that the *Memoirs* is less of an homage to her than to the effect she had on him. He acknowledged that he was charmed by the woman who "studied my tastes, piqued and amused me, challenged frankness by frankness, and did not conceal the good opinion of me she brought with her, nor her wish to please." Because she asked him for his opinions and about his experiences, he admitted it was for him "impossible long to hold out against such urgent assault."[39] Her appeal was to his vanity. Emerson was an easy conquest for Fuller. When he accused her in the *Memoirs* of having a "mountainous ME," he described a woman with a strong self-image who was indeed egoistic, but he also projected his own egotism. Even in learning of her death, Emerson displayed his egocentrism when he mourned in his journal that he had lost his audience. Like any showman, Emerson needed reassurance from an admiring audience. Margaret's brother Richard, describing his visits to the Emerson home, noted that Emerson used to read his lectures aloud by the fireside to his guests. "Elizabeth Hoar used to be there and she acted as a chorus."[40]

Unlike the contributors to the *Memoirs*, Edgar Allan Poe was not emotionally involved with Margaret Fuller, although he was acquainted with her in the New York literary salons they both attended. What is interesting about Poe's criticism of her writing is that he did not make the Emersonian distinction between her conversation and writing; in fact, he wrote that they were "identical." Because Poe is generally accepted as an outstanding American literary critic of the past century, it seems worthwhile to quote his comments at some length:

I put all this as a general proposition, to which Miss Fuller affords a marked exception—to this extent, that her personal character and her printed book are merely one and the same thing. We get access to her soul as directly from the one as from the other—no more readily from this than from that—easily from either. Her acts are bookish, and her books are less thoughts than acts. Her literary and her conversational manner are identical. Here is a passage from her "Summer on the Lakes":—

"The rapids enchanted me far beyond what I expected; they are so swift that they cease to *seem* so—you can think only of their *beauty*. The fountain beyond the Moss islands I discovered for myself, and thought it for some time an *accidental* beauty which it would not do to *leave*, lest I might never see it again. After I found it *permanent*, I returned many times to watch the play of its crest. In the little waterfall beyond, Nature seems, as she often does, to have made a *study* for some larger design. She delights in this—a sketch within a sketch—a dream within a *dream*. Wherever we see it, the lines of the great buttress in the fragment of stone, the hues of the waterfall, copied in the flowers that *star* its bordering mosses, we are *delighted*; for all the lineaments become *fluent*, and we mould the scene in congenial thought with its *genius*."

Now all this is precisely as Miss Fuller would speak it. She is perpetually saying just such things in just such words. To get the conversational woman in the mind's eye, all that is needed is to imagine her reciting the paragraph just quoted; but first let us have the personal woman. She is of medium height; nothing remarkable about the figure; a profusion of lustrous light hair; eyes a bluish gray, full of fire; capacious forehead; the mouth when in repose indicates profound sensibility, capacity for affection, for love—when moved by a slight smile, it becomes even beautiful in the intensity of this expression; but the upper lip, as if impelled by the action of involuntary muscles, habitually uplifts itself, conveying the impression of a sneer. Imagine, now, a person of this description looking you at the moment earnestly in the face, at the next seeming to look only within her own spirit or at the wall; moving nervously every now and then in her chair; speaking in a high key, but musically, deliberately (not hurriedly or loudly), with a delicious distinctness of enunciation—speaking, I say, the paragraph in question, and emphasizing the words which I have italicised, not by impulsion of the breath (as is usual) but by drawing them out as long as possible, nearly closing her eyes the while—imagine all this, and we have both the woman and the authoress before us.[41]

Poe's evaluation is probably more accurate than Emerson's. Stylistic analysis in Chapter 5 will show that her writing method tended to be conversational rather than syllogistic. Moreover, Poe in the same essay acknowledged Fuller's genius—"high genius she unquestionably possesses." He especially praised her review of Longfellow's poetry, a review that was "frank, candid, independent—even ludicrous contrast to the usual mere glorifications of the day," when as Poe pointed out, most critics were toadying to Longfellow's social position and impressed by the fine paper and morocco binding of his books. Even Poe's physical description of Fuller differs from Emerson's. Poe saw her expression as "beautiful" when she had a slight smile. In "Ligeia" Poe used Bacon's quotation that "there is no exquisite beauty without some *strangeness* in the proportion." The energy Margaret generated when she was animated must have made her appear beautiful.

Before "The Literati of New York City"—Poe's impartial judgment of Fuller's writing—appeared in print in August 1846 in

*Godey's Magazine and Lady's Book*, he became enraged with her inter-
ference in one of his personal affairs. At the request of Frances
Osgood, Fuller went with Anne Lynch to his cottage in Fordham to
ask him to return Mrs. Osgood's love letters.[42] Some time after this
incident, in a letter written to George W. Eveleth dated January 4,
1848, Poe described Fuller as "an ill-tempered and very inconsistent
old maid." Fuller's meddlesome behavior is thereby explained by
relegating her to the feminist stereotype.

Henry David Thoreau thought, as Poe did, that Fuller's literary
and conversational manner were identical. In a letter to Fuller in
1843, Emerson wrote: "H. D. Thoreau, who will never like anything, writes 'Miss F's is a noble piece ["The Great Lawsuit"], rich
extempore writing, talking with pen in hand.' "[43] Thoreau also had
an opportunity to be well acquainted with Fuller because they were
both close to the Emerson family in Concord at the same time. Like
other writers, he could not ignore her. In his *A Week on the Concord
and Merrimac Rivers*, he wrote of his feelings:

> I know a woman who possesses a restless and intelligent mind,
> interested in her own culture, and earnest to enjoy the highest
> possible advantages, and I meet her with pleasure as a natural
> person who not a little provokes me, and I suppose is stimu-
> lated in turn by myself. Yet our acquaintance plainly does not
> attain to that degree of confidence and sentiment which
> women, which all, in fact, covet. I am glad to help her, as I am
> helped by her; I like very well to know her with a sort of
> stranger's privilege, and hesitate to visit her often, like her
> other Friends. My nature pauses here, I do not know why.[44]

Thoreau and Poe are two men whose opinions differed from those in
the *Memoirs*. These were men of genius who knew Fuller and who,
unlike the editors of the *Memoirs*, praised the merit of her writing.
But their voices were not heard. Unfortunately, most scholars have
accepted the *Memoirs* as literary dogma instead of adequately considering all of the sources.

Another famous writer of the nineteenth century who was acquainted with Fuller and helped to perpetuate the Fuller feminist
archetype was Thomas Carlyle. In reply to her alleged statement to
him in London in 1846, "I accept the universe," he is supposed to

have retorted, "By Gad, she'd better." As Perry Miller observed in 1963, Americans remember—"if at all"—Margaret Fuller for this exchange.[45]

With the exception of Ralph Waldo Emerson, however, there is no man of letters who was more disturbed by Margaret Fuller than was Nathaniel Hawthorne or who did more to calumniate her reputation. Convincing documentation is available to indicate that Fuller fascinated Hawthorne. In fact he used the Paul Pry method he depicts in his fiction to try to find out more about her love affair with Ossoli. She disturbed him, and he disliked her.[46] He kept trying to exorcise her in his fiction, but her ghost remained. If one were to speculate why, it would probably be because the women in Hawthorne's life (with the exception of Elizabeth Peabody) were withdrawn recluses—polar opposites of Fuller. His mother retired from life while still a young woman when she learned of the death of her husband. His sisters lived quietly, and his chosen bride, Sophia Peabody, was an American version of Elizabeth Barrett, whom he rescued just in time from life as an invalid and restored to health. The whirlwind Fuller, with her suggestion of latent sensuality and her aggressive-dominant personality, was a complete contrast to the pallid ladies he loved.[47]

On the surface Margaret Fuller and Nathaniel Hawthorne were friends. Apparently she liked him as a man and as a writer much better than he did her. His strong reaction to her is reflected in passages from his journal and letters. In November 1840, while still a bachelor, he mentioned in his journal a dinner invitation at George Bancroft's, which he was glad to be able to refuse because of a previous engagement when he learned Fuller was to be a guest. While on Brook Farm on April 13, 1841, he wrote to Sophia Peabody:

> Belovedest, I have not yet taken my first lesson in agriculture, as thou mayest well suppose—except that I went to see our cows foddered, yesterday afternoon. We have eight of our own; and the number is now increased by a transcendental heifer, belonging to Miss Margaret Fuller. She is very fractious, I believe, and apt to kick over the milk pail. Thou knowest best, whether, in these traits of character, she resembles her mistress.

In the last paragraph, he again mentioned Fuller: "Belovedest, Miss Fuller's cow hooks the other cows, and has made herself ruler of the herd, and behaves in a very tyrannical manner."[48]

Paradoxically, after being established with Sophia in Concord, Hawthorne wrote in his journal of an afternoon he spent with Fuller in Sleepy Hollow cemetery: "An old man passed near by and smiled to see Margaret reclining on the ground and me sitting by her side." Hawthorne indicated the old man seemed to think they were lovers. They continued their discussion about the pleasure of being lost in the woods, crows, the influence of childhood upon one's character, mountains, and philosophy. Not until interrupted by Emerson did the talks break up around six o'clock. A few days later he wrote to her declining her suggestion that her married sister board with his family, and after an elaborate explanation for reasons for his refusal, ended the letter with: "There is nobody to whom I would more willingly speak my mind, because I can be certain of being thoroughly understood."[49] If there were any doubt as to the nature of Hawthorne's strange preoccupation with Fuller, publication in 1884 of a new selection from Nathaniel Hawthorne's French and Italian notebooks would make it certain that his feeling was rancor. This portion, written when Hawthorne was in Rome eight years after Fuller's death, was edited by his son, Julian. Hawthorne wrote in his journal:

> Mr. Mozier knew Margaret well, she having been an intimate of his during a part of his residence in Italy. . . . He says that the Ossoli family, though technically noble, is really of no rank whatever; the elder brother, with the title of Marquis, being at this very time a working bricklayer, and the sisters walking the streets without bonnets,—that, is being in the station of peasant-girls. Ossoli himself, to the best of his belief, was _____'s servant, or had something to do with the care of _____'s apartments. He was the handsomest man that Mr. Mozier ever saw, but entirely ignorant, even of his own language; scarcely able to read at all; destitute of manners,—in short, half an idiot, and without any pretension to be a gentleman. . . . He could not possibly have had the least appreciation of Margaret; and the wonder is, what attraction she found in this boor, this man without the intellectual

spark,—she that had always shown such a cruel and bitter scorn of intellectual deficiency. As from her towards him, I do not understand what feeling there could have been; . . . as from him towards her I can understand as little, for she had not the charm of womanhood. But she was a person anxious to try all things, and fill up her experience in all directions; she had a strong and coarse nature, which she had done her utmost to refine, with infinite pains; but of course it could only be superficially changed. The solution of the riddle lies in this direction; nor does one's conscience revolt at the idea of thus solving it; for (at least, this is my own experience) Margaret has not left in the hearts and minds of those who knew her any deep witness of her integrity and purity. She was a great humbug,—of course, with much talent and much moral reality, or else she could never have been so great a humbug. But she had stuck herself full of borrowed qualities, which she chose to provide herself with, but which had no root in her. Mr. Mozier added that Margaret had quite lost all power of literary production before she left Rome, though occasionally the charm and power of her conversation would reappear. To his certain knowledge, she had no important manuscripts with her when she sailed (she having shown him all she had, with a view to his procuring their publication in America), and the "History of the Roman Revolution," about which there was so much lamentation, in the belief that it had been lost with her, never had existence. Thus there appears to have been a total collapse in poor Margaret, morally and intellectually; and, tragic as her catastrophe was, Providence was, after all, kind in putting her and her clownish husband and their child on board that fated ship. There never was such a tragedy as her whole story,—the sadder and sterner, because so much of the ridiculous was mixed up with it, and because she could bear anything better than to be ridiculous. It was such an awful joke, that she should have resolved—in all sincerity, no doubt—to make herself the greatest, wisest, best woman of the age. And to that end she set to work on her strong, heavy, unpliable, and, in many respects, defective and evil nature, and adorned it with a mosaic of admirable qualities, such as she chose to possess; putting in here a splendid talent and there a moral excellence, and polishing each separate piece, and the whole together, till it seemed to shine afar and dazzle all who saw it. She took credit to herself for having been her own Redeemer, if not her own Creator; and, indeed, she was far more a work of art than any of Mozier's statues. But she was not working on an inanimate substance, like marble or clay; there was something within her that she could not possibly come at, to re-create or refine it; and, by and by, this rude old potency bestirred itself, and undid all her labor in the twinkling of an eye. On the whole, I do not know but I like her the better for it; because she proved herself a very woman after all, and fell as the weakest of her sisters might.[50]

The significant point is that Hawthorne chose Mozier to quote rather than the William Wetmore Storys, with whom he was also acquainted. The Storys knew Fuller and her husband much more intimately than did Mozier. But because the Storys were Fuller's chief apologists in Italy, Hawthorne sought a more obscure and negative source. Hawthorne's widow suppressed these malicious comments about Fuller when she released her late husband's journal for publication in 1871. Their son, Julian, however, was not so discreet thirteen years later. Needless to say, this publication aroused indignant rejoinders by Fuller's supporters. From a long-range point of view, the Hawthorne publication is important because it served to keep alive speculation about a personality by then legendary. Controversy continued to center on her life rather than on her writing. From this same journal entry Hawthorne furnished a nucleus of the feminist archetype, which surfaces throughout his fiction.

As has long been recognized, Zenobia is Hawthorne's version of Margaret Fuller in *The Blithedale Romance*. From the time that this work was published until the present day, a discussion of Zenobia inevitably includes some mention of Margaret Fuller—either that her character was or was not based on the prototype Fuller. What is important, however, is that this discussion began as soon as *The Blithedale Romance* was published in 1852—the same year the *Memoirs* appeared. Friends who knew Fuller immediately identified

Zenobia as based on her personality, just as they recognized Blithedale as Brook Farm. As quoted in the letter to his fiancée, Hawthorne made the sly identification of the virgin cow with Fuller, complaining of her "tyrannical" rule of the herd. Because Fuller was a frequent visitor at Brook Farm at the same time that Hawthorne was there (without his beloved Sophia), he seems to have spent a disproportionate amount of time observing her.

Without the testimony or denial of friends, or quotations from letters, there is enough evidence from *The Blithedale Romance* to make the character Zenobia identifiable with Fuller. Although some critics say that Zenobia could have not been based on Margaret Fuller because the character is described as "beautiful," in this respect Hawthorne was merely following the conventional description of a romantic heroine. Moreover in the Coverdale-Hawthorne description of Zenobia, he described her as "an admirable figure of a woman, just on the hither verge of her richest maturity, with a combination of features which it is safe to call remarkably beautiful, even if some fastidious persons might pronounce them a little deficient in softness and delicacy."[51] Hawthorne's qualification of Zenobia's "beauty" is consistent with his later criticisms of Fuller's "strong and coarse" nature. In Coverdale's first meeting with Zenobia, she praises him for his writing (poetry), as Fuller did Hawthorne's fiction. He notices the distinction between Zenobia and other women immediately. Her laugh is "mellow," "not in the least like an ordinary woman's." She then laments women's tedious household tasks, wishing she could exchange places with the men in the field. Coverdale retorts that there were no dinner pots or clothes for Eve to mend in Paradise, whereupon she playfully suggests that it is too cold to wear "the garb of Eden." Coverdale muses ironically: "Assuredly, Zenobia could not have intended it," but from her words and manner, he begins to wonder how her "fine, perfectly developed figure" would look in "Eve's earliest garment." Descriptions of Margaret Fuller indicate that her figure was well developed. Furthermore Hawthorne recorded Fuller's nurturing of him while he was ill at Brook Farm through Coverdale's response to Zenobia's doing likewise: she added "several gratuitous throbs to my pulse."

Through Coverdale's insistent prying, he tries to confirm his suspicion of Zenobia's secret sin—smouldering sensuality. After associating her with Eve, he compares her to Pandora, full of "celestial warmth," and later with the feminist stereotype, "a witch," with "some magical property in the flower that you wear in your hair." Fuller frequently adorned her hair with a flower. Hawthorne's Zenobia has Fuller's "abundant" hair, but he has changed her fair hair to dark, thus conforming to the dark lady convention in literature.

If the Zenobia-Fuller parallel were merely based on their corresponding sensuality, the identification of Fuller as Zenobia would not necessarily be clear. The comparison of Zenobia to royalty provides proof that Fuller was her prototype. Descriptions in the *Memoirs* compare Fuller with a queen; Emerson quoted the phrase—"*Incedit regina*"—that her father used to describe her and wrote: "I have heard, that from the beginning of her life, she idealized herself as a sovereign."[52] If this royal identification were not reiterated in the *Memoirs*, it must also be remembered that the epigraph to *Woman in the Nineteenth Century* is, "The earth waits for her queen." Hawthorne and his wife had read this work, and thus he, as did so many of Fuller's friends, identified her with her epigraph.[53] As delineated in the novel, Zenobia was the pen name, "the magazine signature," not the true name of this woman. Because Fuller's work had been frequently published, the fact that Zenobia was an author further contributes to this theory. In addition, Hawthorne's choice of the name Zenobia is significant. The biblical Tadmor, after the revolt in 273 A.D. of its queen, Zenobia, was destroyed by the emperor Aurelian. Hawthorne said of Zenobia: she "had as much native pride as any queen would have known what to do with." Again he described "the queenliness of her presence" and her behavior "as the act of a queen."

Besides her royal bearing, another characteristic of Margaret Zenobia is her dramatic ability. As Horace Greeley once observed, had Fuller "condescended to appear before the footlights, she would have been recognized as the first actress of the Nineteenth Century."[54] Or as Hawthorne expressed it in his notebooks, Fuller was a "great humbug," with "borrowed qualities." Zenobia, too, exhibited dramatic ability, giving readings from Shakespeare (which Fuller loved), so that it was an "intolerable wrong to the world that she did not at once go upon the stage."

In what sounds almost like a reiteration of Emerson's comments relative to Fuller's writing ability, Coverdale says of Zenobia: "Her poor little stories and tracts never half did justice to her intellect. It was only the lack of a fitter avenue that drove her to seek development in literature." To make this parallel unmistakable Zenobia says: "But the pen is not for woman. . . . It is with the living voice alone that she can compel the world to recognize the light of her intellect and the depth of her heart!" Just as in the picture of Fuller in the *Memoirs*, Zenobia can talk better than she can write.

If there were any mistakes as to Hawthorne's portrait, Zenobia favors women's rights; she has written tracts in defense of her sex. Even in death, her hands were clenched in "never-ending hostility, immitigable defiance." And the mode of her death by drowning parallels Fuller's death at sea.

If Zenobia is a portrait of Margaret Fuller, a reader might ask why Hawthorne specifically mentioned that his heroine, Priscilla, resembles Margaret Fuller, "a friend of mine, one of the most gifted women of the age. . . . a certain curve of the shoulders, and a partial closing of the eyes." The answer might be that this is an expression of the sly humor of Hawthorne. Realizing his sketch of Zenobia too closely paralleled Fuller, he may have written this as a deliberate device to confuse his readers. Whatever else it suggests, it is significant that he mentioned Fuller by name in this novel.

From the many parallels of the life of Margaret Fuller and her legend created in the *Memoirs*, it is evident that Hawthorne had her in mind when writing *The Blithedale Romance*. What also needs to be pointed out is that the Snow Maiden wins the man in the love triangle with Zenobia. Hawthorne's portrait of the weak, passive, "Miss Goody Two Shoes," Priscilla (the antithesis of Zenobia) was fair warning to generations of young women that if they wanted a man, they had better not be in favor of women's rights. And he ended his romance with a final joke: the voyeur Coverdale confesses that he, too, loved Priscilla. The only consolation for Zenobia is her threat before her death that she would haunt the man who had rejected her, as in truth Fuller haunted Hawthorne.

Indeed Fuller/Zenobia did haunt Hawthorne, because some years later she reappeared as his Miriam in *The Marble Faun*. The character Donatello (who represents the handsome Marchese Giovanni Angelo Ossoli) is brought to his moral destruction by Miriam. This novel contains the usual Hawthornian trappings. There is Miriam, the woman with a sinful past. Hilda, another Snow Maiden, plays opposite Miriam. The parallels with the romance of the Ossolis are significant. Miriam picks up Donatello, who has been following her, as Fuller picked up Ossoli in St. Peter's basilica. Donatello is strikingly handsome, as was Ossoli. ("He was the handsomest man that Mr. Mozier ever saw.") Both the fictional character and Ossoli were Italian and younger than their ladies. Hawthorne had commented on what he believed to be Ossoli's ignorance and near illiteracy, and he depicts Donatello as having a strain of the animal fawn in him—"as gentle and docile as a pet spaniel"—a simple uneducated man beneath Miriam in culture. Again Miriam is something of an actress with personal magnetism: "You have bewitched the poor lad." And Miriam is beautiful and queenly, "arrayed in queenly robes," with a "natural self-reliance." Kenyon, the sculptor (Coverdale-Dimmesdale), is shocked to see "how Miriam's rich, ill-regulated nature impelled her to fling herself, conscience and all, on one passion, the object of which intellectually seemed far beneath her." In this novel, Miriam, who like Fuller had fallen "as the weakest of her sisters," is as "evil" as Hawthorne said Fuller was, as she "with her eyes" tells Donatello to kill her tormentor. Again as with Zenobia, it is a case of hubris getting its due as Miriam confesses: "I used to fancy that, at my need, I could bring the whole world to my feet. And lo! here is my utmost need; and my beauty and my gifts have brought me only this poor, simple boy. Half-witted, they call him." Ossoli the clown has been transfigured into the half-wit faun despite the fact that he is a young count. Miriam, "the guilty, blood-stained, lonely woman," had corrupted the "innocent, whom she had drawn into her doom." What seems evident here is that again Hawthorne depicted the feminist archetype with her tainted past as a destructive person. Only the pure Hilda, who does not create art but merely copies it, is rewarded with a husband—the happy ending.

Hawthorne's same obsessive theme of evil, which he represented by female fall from virtue, is earlier depicted in his classic *The Scarlet Letter*. Because he brought in the women's rights issue so late in the romance, not many people pay much attention to it. At the end of *The Scarlet Letter*, published the year of Fuller's death, but with time enough for him to have learned of her "fall," Hawthorne wrote: "a new truth would be revealed, in order to establish the whole relation between man and woman on a surer ground of mutual happiness. Earlier in life, Hester had vainly imagined that she herself might be the destined prophetess, but had long since recognized the impossibility that any mission of divine and mysterious truth should be confided to a woman stained with sin."

Even Hester's thwarted dream of being the "destined prophetess" has some association with the image that Fuller presented to the transcendental circle. The Hawthorne heroines reflect a Promethian female, who dared to challenge the masculine gods in their pride and in their sexual desire, who envied man's position of power and wanted to usurp his privileges. Fallen women all—from Hester who redeems herself, to Zenobia who destroys herself, to Miriam who destroys others—there is a decline in the virtue of the woman. With Miriam there is no consolation of felix culpa as Hester had—only the emptiness of recognizing that she has been a Circe-Lamia. Hawthorne's novels seem to be exorcising his witch, whom he had met in the flesh in the person of Margaret Fuller.[55] In *The Blithedale Romance* Hawthorne best described himself: "That cold tendency between instinct and intellect, which makes me pry with a speculative interest into people's passions and impulses, appeared to have gone far towards unhumanizing my heart." His obsessive fascination persisted long after Fuller's death. Hawthorne extended the feminist archetype created in the *Memoirs* to fictional representations of the fallen woman.

Oliver Wendell Holmes continued the onslaught against the threatening feminist personified by Margaret Fuller. As children, he and Fuller attended the same school. Later when he was a student at Harvard, he kept up his acquaintance with her. Unlike Hawthorne, some of his harsh judgements were softened by time. Reminiscing at the age of sixty, he doubted if he had ever judged her fairly and wished he could have the opportunity to talk to her again in their old age. In his essay, "Cinders from the Ashes," he wryly explained that she made him feel inadequate when he read one of her school themes, which began, "It is a trite remark." He did not know then what *trite* meant and later asked: "How could I ever judge Margaret fairly after such a crushing discovery of her superiority?" Her manner to the other children was proudly aloof: "Her air to her schoolmates was marked by a certain stateliness and distance, as if she had other thoughts than theirs and was not of them. She was a great student and a great reader of what she used to call *naw-vels*." He then gave a description of her appearance as he recalled it:

> I remember her so well as she appeared at school and later, that I regret that she had not been faithfully given to canvas or marble in the day of her best looks. None know her aspect who have not seen her living. Margaret, as I remember her at school and afterwards, was tall, fair complexioned, with a watery, aqua-marine lustre in her light eyes, which she used to make small, as one does who looks at the sunshine. A remarkable point about her was that long, flexile neck, arching and un-dulating in strange sinuous movements, which one who loved her would compare to those of a swan, and one who loved her not to those of the ophidian who tempted our common mother. Her talk was affluent, magisterial, *de haut en bas*, some would say euphuistic, but surpassing the talk of women in breadth and audacity. Her face kindled and reddened and dilated in every feature as she spoke, and, as I once saw her in fine storm of indignation at the supposed ill-treatment of a relative, showed itself capable of something resembling what Milton calls the viraginian aspect.[56]

What is especially interesting about Holmes's description of Fuller is that although he claimed to have remembered her "so well," his account closely mirrored Channing's in the *Memoirs*. Channing wrote:

> She certainly had not beauty; yet the high arched dome of the head, the changeful expressiveness of every feature, and her whole air of mingled dignity and impulse, gave her a com-manding charm. Especially characteristic were two physical traits. The first was a contraction of the eyelids almost to a point,—a trick caught from near-sightedness,—and then a sudden dilation, till the iris seemed to emit flashes;—an effect, no doubt, dependent on her highly-magnetized condition. The second was a singular pliancy of the vertebrae and mus-cles of the neck, enabling her by a mere movement to denote each varying emotion; moments of tenderness, or pensive

feeling, its curves were swan-like in grace, but when she was scornful or indignant it contracted, and made swift turns like that of a bird of prey. Finally, in the animation, yet *abandon* of Margaret's attitude and look, were rarely blended the fiery force of northern, and the soft languor of southern races.[57]

In a comparison of the two descriptions of her neck, it is significant that both men used the image of the swan, but Holmes changed Channing's "bird of prey" to the "ophidian," who tempted Eve. Both versions contain references to her contracting eyelids and to her animated manner.

Holmes also incorporated aspects of Margaret Fuller in his *Elsie Venner* (1858–1859) and *A Mortal Antipathy* (1885). These novels are little known today, and what interest they still arouse is mainly in the field of psychology. A book-length study, *The Psychiatric Novels of Oliver Wendell Holmes* by Clarence P. Oberndorf, a clinical professor of psychiatry at Columbia University, says that his "medicated novels" contain material indicating he was a precursor of Freud and Jung. The concept of the importance of prenatal influence in the development of a person is explored in *Elsie Venner: A Romance of Destiny*. The way that Holmes presented this idea is by having Elsie's mother bitten by a snake during pregnancy. He suggested that Elsie had been poisoned before birth and hence was not responsible for her actions. Holmes developed this concept by means of the character Elsie Venner. Although the Venner-Fuller parallel is suggested by the similarity of their last names, it is sustained in the description of Elsie, which echoes the Channing-Holmes description of Margaret's eyes and neck: "She [Elsie] narrowed her lids slightly, as one often sees a sleepy cat narrow hers,—somewhat as you may remember our famous Margaret used to, if you remember her at all,—so that her eyes looked very small, but bright as the diamonds on her breast."[58]

In addition to her physical attributes, Elsie Venner suggests Fuller by her personality. She possesses magnetic qualities, which either attract or repel those around her. Because she is so enigmatic, he says she "would have been burned for a witch in old times." Her aloof and lonely nature possesses marks of genius, poetic or dramatic. She also is a woman of violent emotions, who suffers frequent headaches as did Fuller. When thwarted, she reacts in a similar manner to Fuller's autobiographical "Mariana": Elsie locks her door and throws herself to the floor in violent convulsions. The fact that Holmes changed Channing's description of Fuller's neck movement from "bird of prey" to "ophidian" makes Elsie's description more evil and fit in with the snake, symbolic of original sin. In his essay written some ten years after his novel, Holmes specifically described Fuller's neck as "ophidian." Like the ending of Hawthorne's novels, there is to be no happiness for the strange, proud woman. When Elsie is rejected by the man she loves, she pines for him and dies at the end of the novel because she refuses all food.

In another psychological novel that deals with the unconscious and phobias, *A Mortal Antipathy*, written sixteen years later, Holmes presented another heroine who has some resemblance to Fuller. Dr. Oberndorf points out the parallel between the feminist character, Lurida Vincent, and Margaret Fuller:

> In the literary group which Holmes dominated with all the force of a realist was the sharp-witted, overeducated, rather generally disliked Margaret Fuller. When she was born her mother had prayed that 'she would have Timothy's [her father's] mind.' Holmes had known her since childhood. Margaret Fuller, whose life strivings were strongly determined by an envy of man's intellectual achievements, might well have served as a pattern for Lurida.[59]

Lurida is dubbed "The Terror" in *A Mortal Antipathy* because she is the leader of the "advocates of virile womanhood"; in other words she is a suffragette, who manages to get herself elected secretary of the Pansophian Society. She is described as being aggressive and sometimes irritating, whereas her counterpart, Euthymia Tower, has the necessary attributes of a lady—a "restful and sympathetic nature." When Lurida talks to the doctor, she asks him to talk to her as if she "were a man, a grown man." It must be remembered that Holmes was a doctor, so, Dr. Butts, his alter ego in the novel, gives his views:

> Again the doctor felt it his duty to guard Lurida against indiscretions into which her theory of the equality, almost the identity, of the sexes might betray her. Too much of the

woman in a daughter of our race leads her to forget danger—too little prompts her to defy it. Fortunately this last class of women are not quite so likely to be perilously seductive as their more emphatically feminine sisters.

Dr. Butts also warns Lurida against advising Euthymia to become a doctor:

I am disposed to agree that you will often spoil a good nurse to make a poor doctor. I am for giving women every chance for a good education, and if they think medicine is one of their proper callings to let them try it. The trouble is that they are so impressible and imaginative that they are at the mercy of all sorts of fancy systems. Charlatanism always hobbled on two crutches, the tattle of women and the certificates of clergy-men, and I am afraid that half the women doctors will be too much under those influences.

With Holmes's expressed anti-feminism, it is not difficult to surmise who would win the contest for the hero, Maurice Kirk-wood. The hero has an abnormal fear of women and is further frightened by Lurida, who makes the mistake of being too aggres-sive and writing a letter to him. Then in a crisis when the hero is trapped in a burning building, the feminist Lurida faints, whereas Euthymia manages to rescue him and cure him of his phobia. The difference between *A Mortal Antipathy* and *Elsie Venner*, or *The Blithedale Romance*, however, is that the frustrated feminist does not kill herself for love; instead she finds another man. This softens the ending somewhat; nevertheless, Holmes used the stereotype of the feminist as a terror—an unattractive woman. So Holmes, like Hawthorne before him, was so repelled by Margaret Fuller that he turned to his pen to dispose of her haunting influence on his life. Holmes was milder than Hawthorne, but the influence of the *Memoirs* on his description of Fuller in both his recollection of her and his fictional portrayal of feminists is marked.

Unlike Holmes, Henry James was of the generation that did not know Margaret Fuller. But he heard about her for the first time as a child of seven when Washington Irving told him of her death. From that time on, what he was later to refer to as the "Margaret-ghost" continued to haunt him. And he seemed perplexed about what to do with her. Although Fuller did not fit into his category of doomed, innocent, or suffering but brave lady, he finally seized upon one aspect of the Fuller canon from the *Memoirs* and narrowed it into a caricature of the feminist as lesbian. He accelerated the process of accretion that was already at work with the Fuller-inspired archetype.

In James's *The Bostonians* (1886), he satirized women associated with the feminist movement. Verena Tarrant (an emotional and inspiring speaker) and Mrs. Farrinder (the great apostle of the emancipation of women, who lives at Roxbury), possess aspects of the feminist archetype, but Olive Chancellor is the feminist whose portrait is most likely to have been inspired by the Fuller canon. Again she has the strange eyes attributed to Fuller: "The curious tint of her eyes was a living colour; when she turned it upon you, you thought vaguely of the glitter of green ice."[60] And, like Emerson's Fuller, "She was not so plain on further acquaintance as she had seemed to him at first." Sexually she is "a signal old maid." "She was a spinster as Shelley was a lyric poet." Like Fuller, she read German and especially liked Goethe. Her view of history was to study the "long martyrdom of women" and the cruel tyranny of men. She is emotional and takes "things hard." Although contention "always cost her tears, headaches, a day or two in bed," Olive Chancellor still found "of all things in the world contention was most sweet." Early she recognizes Basil Ransom as her adversary. He considers "universal sisterhood" and "the further stultification of the suffrage, the prospect of conscript mothers in the national Senate," ridiculous. As usual with novels concerning feminism, there is a triangle composed of two women and one man. Instead of the usual competition for the man, Olive Chancellor and Basil Ransom are in a contest to win Verena Tarrant. Verena, a poor descendant of abolitionists, has inherited the inspired tongue of her grandfather and has been lecturing for women's rights under the tutelage of her patron, Olive Chancellor. Because the two women live together, Verena wants to prove to the world that "a woman *could* live on persistently, clinging to a great, vivifying, redemptory idea, without the help of a man." On the night that is to be her greatest triumph before a packed music hall audience, she is scheduled to lecture on "A Woman's Reason." Instead of giving her lecture, she elopes with the handsome south-erner, Basil Ransom, who was a former slave owner and officer in the Confederate army. Before their marriage, Basil makes it clear that he does not want his wife "to think too much"; he wants her to be "private and passive." Verena is crying as she flees the au-ditorium, and the last words of the omniscient James are that her tears were not the last "she was destined to shed." This strange switch on the usual happy ending comes as somewhat of a surprise, although it is no surprise that the feminist is again the loser.

Seventeen years after publication of *The Bostonians*, Henry James was still wondering why the "Margaret-ghost" haunted him. If she were alive, he speculated for the "amusement of evocation," would she have been a candidate for "the cosmopolite crowns"? For, he wrote echoing the *Memoirs*, "her written utterance being naught," would she, "with her appetite for ideas and her genius for conversa-tion, have struck us but as a somewhat formidable bore," or as a New England Corinne? He thought for all her "conceit" she might have been surprised to know that half a century after her death, she was still talked about.[61] In the huge spiderweb of James's uncon-scious, something was lost. He did not manage to guess the unseen from the seen or to find the look from the Margaret-ghost that would convey her meaning. Essentially what he achieved with his laughter in *The Bostonians* was another layering in the Fuller archetype: the modern caricature of the feminist as unhappy lesbian. And Verena's decision to choose love in a precipitous flight from her commitment to her speaking career was the germ of many twentieth-century Hollywood productions.

The Fuller castigation was set not only in fiction but in poetry as well. In James Russell Lowell's *A Fable for Critics* (1848), Fuller is satirized under her persona, "Miranda," along with Whittier, Emer-son, Hawthorne, and others. What is interesting, though, is that Lowell's satire against Fuller is much more Juvenalian than the satires against the other writers. In his verse, Lowell attacked her for her spite, egoism, her sibylline tone, reliance on the Infinite Soul, and writing. Probably Emerson derived his "mountainous ME" from Lowell's lines in this poem, written four years before the *Memoirs*:

> And she well may defy any mortal to see through it.
> When once she has mixed up her infinite *me* through it.

He described her writing:

> I'm as much out of salt as Miranda's own writings

And Carlyle's sarcastic remark about Fuller accepting the universe echoes:

> Miranda meanwhile has succeeded in driving
> Up to a corner, in spite of their striving,
> A small flock of tearful victims, and there,
> With an I-turn-the-crank-of-the-Universe air
> And a tone which, at least to *my* fancy, appears
> Not so much to be entering as boxing your ears,
> Is unfolding a tale (of herself, I surmise,
> For 't is dotted as thick as a peacock's with I's.).

One of the "tearful victims" was James Russell Lowell, whose invective was due to her literary review of his poetry. In her essay, "American Literature" (1846), she said Lowell's verse was stereotyped and "wanting in the true spirit and tone of poesy." Lowell found it difficult to forget her review. Continuing his sallies in a letter to William Wetmore Story, Lowell wrote on March 10, 1848:

> There must be not a little of the desolate island where S. M. F. is considered agreeable. . . . I have it on good authority that the Austrian Government has its eye on Miss F. It would be a pity to have so much worth and genius shut up for life in Spielberg. Her beauty might perhaps save her. Pio Nono also regards her with a naturally jealous eye, fearing that the College of Cardinals may make her the successor of Pope Joan.[62]

Fuller concluded her evaluation of Lowell by saying that "his thought sounds no depth; and posterity will not remember him."

Although Lowell is not popularly known today, he was one of the most influential literary figures of his century. Her prognostication was shocking but accurate. After early attempts at writing poetry, he became the first editor of the *Atlantic Monthly*, a lecturer, a Harvard professor, British ambassador, and in a long life (1819–1891), he exerted great influence on the thought of his age. He laid the groundwork for the myth of the spiteful, egotistic feminist through his bitter satire against Margaret Fuller.

Few people in the field of letters dared to disagree with the Fuller canon. Least of all to disagree with opinion was Sarah Josepha Hale, editor of the first women's periodical, the *Ladies' Magazine*, which began publication in 1828. An opponent of the ballot for women, Hale was one of the most influential women of her day, and in *Women's Record* (1855), she gave utterance to established opinion about Margaret Fuller:

> Whatever she might have done, we are constrained to add, that of the books she has left, we do not believe that they are destined to hold a high place in female literature. There is no true moral life in them. . . . But the genius of Margaret Fuller will live only while the tender remembrance of personal friendship shall hold it dear. Her fame, like that of a great actor, or singer, was dependent on her living presence,— gained more by her conversational powers than by her writing.[63]

Margaret's brother, Arthur, continued the distortion begun by the editors of the *Memoirs* in his introductions to posthumous editions of her work. He said that friends felt her words were more eloquent than her pen. In fact, he praised the *Memoirs* as "a work I cannot too warmly recommend to those who would know my sister's character."[64] Moreover, as an ordained minister, he felt it necessary to emphasize his sister's Christian faith in his preface to an edition of *Woman* published in 1855: "God seemed nearer to her than to any person I have ever known. . . . Jesus, the friend of man, can never have been more truly loved and honored than she loved and honored him." Not recognizing the irony of the fact that he was writing a preface to a feminist manifesto, Fuller's brother was at pains to reassure his readers that despite his sister's intellectual accomplishments, she did not neglect a woman's domestic duties, no matter how humble.

Almost thirty years later, Julia Ward Howe, who had attended Fuller's conversations, wrote the first of the many biographies that were to follow. Instead of concentrating on Fuller's literary production, the biographers continued the cult of personality, either as a reiteration of or criticism of concepts that had been set in motion by the *Memoirs*. Written for the Little, Brown Famous Women Series, Howe's biography focuses on the theme appropriate to the series—why Fuller was famous—as a means of educating young readers. Probably because an aura of scandal still lingered, Howe devoted much of her prefatory note to an explanation of the reason she chose to call the biography "Margaret Fuller" rather than "Margaret Fuller Ossoli." Moreover, because this famous author of "The Battle Hymn of the Republic" was a member of the Radical Club in Boston, an editor with her husband of the antislavery paper, *Commonwealth*, and a lecturer on woman's suffrage, prison reform, and international peace, it would be expected that she would emphasize Fuller's feminist writing. However, she did not. She explained briefly that she could not give extended notice of *Woman*, although she paraphrased some of its arguments and observed that its teaching was still appropriate.[65]

Twenty years after the publication of her biography, Julia Ward Howe edited Fuller's love letters to James Nathan, which express a love he did not return. In her introduction, Howe wrote: "The literary material which she left behind her appears small in dimension, when thought of in comparison with the scope of her intellect and the height of her aspiration." Julia Ward Howe concluded her introduction to these letters with the observation that Margaret's disappointment did not "darken the glowing interpretation of life and its conditions, which was her best gift to the men and women of her time, and of our own as well."[66] Over the span of twenty years, Julia Ward Howe still reflected the Fuller canon: she was inspiring as a personality rather than as a writer.

The year 1884 saw the publication of another biography of Fuller, this one by the distinguished man of letters and liberal thinker, Thomas Wentworth Higginson, who is largely remembered today for encouraging the poet Emily Dickinson. Although as a child he

was acquainted with Fuller and was a friend of her younger
brothers, he stated in his introduction that he considered his biography an intermediate step between the *Memoirs*, "which gave the
estimate offered by personal friendship—and that remoter verdict
which will be the judgment of an impartial posterity." Recognizing
that he could not be objective, he wrote that except for Emerson,
and possibly Theodore Parker, Fuller had upon him a more immediate intellectual influence through her writing than anyone else.
Hence he was circumspect in his remarks as he suggested that the
judgment of the *Memoirs* leaves Fuller "too much in the clouds," that
her life was not merely a quest for self-culture but rather an expression of thought mingled with action. Viewing her life as a whole,
Higginson tended to concentrate on its action. When he did comment on her writing, it was to defend her criticism. Despite her
unpopular reviews of Longfellow and Lowell that he thought were
"less than just," Higginson called her "the best literary critic whom
America has yet seen." In addition to praising her "lyric glimpses,"
he found some development of proper control in her writing style
but considered *Woman* "discursive and unmethodical."[67] Nevertheless, Higginson devoted much of his discussion to a defense of
Fuller's personality, arguing that she was not unduly vain and
self-absorbed. Higginson should be given credit for recognizing the
unfair portrait that the *Memoirs* painted. Although more objective in
its analysis, his biography is, as Higginson said, an intermediate
step.[68]

An example of the type of personal attack that Higginson was
trying to counteract was that by William Morton Payne, who
twenty years after Higginson's biography wrote: "It was characteristic of Margaret Fuller's mind to view 'with satisfaction' her own
achievements. Self-consciousness and the Sibylline pose are everywhere manifest in her writings."[69]

In 1895, Caroline W. Healey, in *Margaret and Her Friends*, recon-
structed from her notes some of Fuller's famous conversations,
which Healey had attended as a young woman. The theme of the
conversations is mythology, and no direct discussion of female
emancipation is recorded. What has been largely overlooked, however, is Healey's preface in which she said Margaret's mother and
brother Richard had wanted her to write a biography that would

"put an end to many absurd and painful rumors which had followed the publication of the first *Memoir*." This account, to be printed at the family's expense, was not written due to Richard's death. What is important here is that Fuller's surviving relatives recognized the damage that the *Memoirs* had done to her reputation.

Twentieth-century biographies—*Margaret Fuller, A Psychological Biography* (1920) by Katharine Anthony, *Margaret Fuller* (1930) by Margaret Bell, *Margaret Fuller: Whetstone of Genius* (1940) by Mason Wade, *The Life of Margaret Fuller* (1942) by Madeleine Stern, and *In Quest of Love* (1957) by Faith Chipperfield—mention *Woman*'s influence on the feminist movement. These biographies are primarily concerned with Fuller as a powerful personality rather than as a writer. Stern's very readable biography is a re-creation of Fuller in her milieu and times, whereas Wade's concerns Fuller's role as a catalyst in American intellectual life, with *Woman* designated as a tract for the times. Even the unconventional Eleanor Roosevelt, who wrote an introduction to Margaret Bell's biography, accepted the established opinion when discussing Fuller's contribution: "It is not what she wrote which makes her life for us a vivid influence to-day, but what she was, and in this book, from a rather tragic childhood to the heroic and tragic end, you feel the sweep of a great personality."[70]

Twentieth-century scholars have carried to the academic world the Fuller myth of the *Memoirs*. In 1917, the prestigious *Cambridge History of American Literature* discussed the Fuller personality:

She could use her tongue sharply and sarcastically, a quality which, combined with a high temper and a tendency to tell the truth, made her many enemies; and gradually as she became more widely known, out of these hints that she herself supplied, there emerged in the public mind a distorted conception of her personality—a view that still lingers— which made her out a woman of insufferable vanity and masculinity, a veritable intellectual virago.

The editors continued by saying that "along with Alcott she became a chief butt of coarse and unsympathetic critics."[71] The editors of this reference book, which was used by generations of students, also recognized the distortion of Fuller's personality but suggested that it was due to the "hints" she supplied. And as de rigueur, discussion is concerned with her personality rather than with her writing. In a July 1949 issue of *Harper's Magazine*, Edward Nicholas published an article with a title that reveals its context: "It Is I: Margaret Fuller." Pointing out her egotism and audacity, he reiterated the tired line that she was a great conversationalist rather than a writer and, with a bit of Hawthorne's bias, observed that she found Ossoli "unlettered and poor." Still he wondered why Ossoli was attracted to "the American woman with the sad plain face, ten years older." In 1951, Arthur Hobson Quinn in his frequently consulted literary history observed that Fuller represented transcendentalism "on its emotional side."[72]

But it was Perry Miller (1905–1963), with impressive credentials as a professor of American literature at Harvard and the author of numerous scholarly books, who gave the academic stamp to the Lowell-Emerson-Hawthorne creation. In an article with a title quoted from the *Memoirs*, "I Find No Intellect Comparable to My Own," Miller intensified the distortion of the feminist archetype. He selected the most derogatory descriptions of Fuller's appearance that he could find to quote and changed former descriptions of her full figure to "angular and ailing," descriptions of her abundant hair to "not quite blond, stringy, and thin," and asserted that she was "phenomenally homely." He further disregarded Emerson's remarks about Fuller's "drolleries" and joy, that made him laugh more than he would have liked, to assert that she was a woman without a sense of humor. He accepted the emotional aspects of the Fuller canon: "her style [was] as verbose as her emotions were chaotic." And like Hawthorne, Miller found Fuller ridiculous:

> The temptation to make Margaret a great liberal, a champion for the splendid proposition that women have a right to possess and use intelligence, and to shed tears over her untimely death, is too often offset by the suspicion that Nathaniel Hawthorne was in some degree correct when he said that much of the ridiculous was mixed up with her tragedy. The long neck, the nearsighted arrogance, whose qualities which put her in the *galerie* of the bluestockings of that age, like them (in James' phrase) "glossily ringletted and monumentally breastpinned," prevent us from erecting memorials.[73]

Miller's reasoning here is not clear. Apparently he could not forgive Fuller for being ugly. After illustrating his article with a reproduction of a picture from an 1867 issue of *Leslie's* magazine, he wrote in his caption that the popular magazine "romanticizing the tragic last act, her death by shipwreck, made the aging, unlovely Margaret young and beautiful."[74] He also said she seemed ludicrous, although he did not make it clear why. In another instance, he tried to explain why he thought she was funny: "One factor in our settling a public image of Margaret Fuller is that she cannot be dissociated from the hyperbolically female intellectualism of the period, the slightest invocation of which invites our laughter." The fact that Miller chose to incorporate the Lowell-Hawthorne-James ridicule to his evaluation of Fuller is important. If the feminist archetype is funny rather than tragic, converts to her cause are few. He also accepted Hawthorne's evaluation of Ossoli's intelligence and credentials—"some vague claim to being a marquis"—to diminish Fuller's stature further or to make her appear more ridiculous.

When Miller discussed her writing in *Woman*, he complained of its "lofty . . . hysterical" level because it "can hardly stoop to argue the mundane business of the ballot." An additional fault of her prose, he found, was that it is turgid: "The dithrambic prolixity of her writings, quickly came to seem, to the few who looked at them embarrassing." During 1963, Perry Miller also issued an anthology of Fuller's work, in which he expanded some of his ideas presented in the *American Heritage* article. Of *Woman*, he said: "It is full of wearisome digressions and excursions into fantasy and murky dreams, and the thread of the discourse is frequently lost." Miller observed further that her feminist propaganda was a slight contribution to the campaign for women's rights. The reason why Fuller had not been forgotten, Miller wrote, was that she was the "only candidate" for the "role of a native champion of the Romantic heroine in the grandoise (and so, for an American dangerously close to the ludicrous) operatic manner."[75] After giving her due credit for her ability as a critic and an intellectual, Miller concluded that her achievement as a role player was what had kept her memory alive. Because Miller acknowledged that "the indispensable source book for the study of the life and mind of Margaret Fuller" was the *Memoirs*, there is no doubt that he had partaken of the ambivalence of its editors. Moreover, he added "ridiculous" to the Fuller canon, thus giving scholarly credence to the term first used by Hawthorne.

James Russell Lowell, Ralph Waldo Emerson, Nathaniel Hawthorne, Oliver Wendell Holmes, and Perry Miller all reacted to Margaret Fuller in an unwitting conspiracy of outrage. Threatened, they used their pens like a chorus to denigrate Fuller as an intellectual and as a writer. Not until the Fuller feminist archetype is discarded can an objective study of Margaret Fuller as a writer be made. The best account of what happened to Fuller's reputation was given indirectly by the suffragettes who edited the *History of Woman Suffrage*. They said all of the world's literature is used to assert woman's inferiority: "And not only do such women suffer these ever-recurring indignities in daily life, but the literature of the world proclaims their inferiority and divinely decreed subjection in all history, sacred and profane, in science, philosophy, poetry and song."[76] Fuller made it clear in *Woman* that she understood the propaganda value of literature as a way of influencing woman's behavior and values.

As a visionary, Fuller would have understood what happened to her reputation. In fact, she prophesied that she would encounter hostility for as long as she lived: "Eternity is with us, but there is much darkness and bitterness in this portion of it. A baleful star rose on my birth, and its hostility, I fear, will never be disarmed while I walk below."[77] Hostility from her "baleful star" continued to follow her long after death.

In an effort to ascertain the truth, Joseph Jay Deiss, in his *The Roman Years of Margaret Fuller*, was the first biographer to make a thorough investigation of the last four years of her life, which she spent in Europe. His major concern was with her life in Italy, which was so crucially important to her reputation. Because he knew Italy well (he lived there for a number of years and spoke and read Italian), Deiss was able to do some significant original research. He settled the question that Hawthorne raised as to the authenticity of the nobility of the Ossoli family. His investigation of the Ossoli della Torre family reveals that the name was recorded in the Golden Book of Italian Nobility. Originating in the north near Lake Garda in the early Middle Ages, the Ossoli family had moved to Rome and the papal service by 1685. Deiss investigated thoroughly the problem that had concerned friends, enemies, and biographers ever since her marriage was first announced: to determine when, where, or if she had married the Marchese Giovanni Angelo Ossoli.[78]

It is hoped that whether Margaret Fuller was legally married is no longer relevant to an analysis of her writing. As late as December 20, 1969, a writer in the *Saturday Review* used the occasion of reviewing the Deiss biography to assert that Fuller's story contains "useful morals for disciples of Betty Friedan." Inexplicably, she compared as a good example of a prudent woman the wife of Secretary of State William Rogers, who chose to marry instead of taking the bar exams, to Fuller with her "need for love and its consequences."[79] Although Fuller conceded that a woman is more likely to inspire than to create art, she did not argue that a need for love necessarily excludes a need for a woman's intellectual and spiritual development.

No doubt the power of Margaret Fuller's complex personality will continue to arouse interest. Women who do not wish to disguise their intelligence or ambition will continue to identify with her, and people who prefer women who play their traditional roles will continue to feel threatened by her.

What needs to be recognized is that the Fuller legend should no longer take precedence over actually reading what Fuller has to say. It is no accident that critics have been able to look at her literary criticism with more objectivity than at her feminist manifesto. It is time that a dispassionate judgment of *Woman in the Nineteenth Century* is made—an analysis free from the distortion and subsequent myth surrounding Margaret Fuller's personality, which have prevented such a study from appearing.

In order to evaluate the extent of Fuller's contribution, it is first desirable to determine how original her thinking was and how she reshaped ideas from many sources. The late eighteenth-century radical thought emanating from the Age of the Enlightenment provided great intellectual stimulation for her inquiring mind.

## NOTES

1. Henry James, *William Wetmore Story and His Friends* (1903; rpt., New York: Grove Press), 1:127.

2. Ida Husted Harper, *The Life and Works of Susan B. Anthony* (Indianapolis: Hollenbeck Press, 1898), 1:131.

3. Margaret Fuller Ossoli, *Woman in the Nineteenth Century and Kindred Papers Related to the Sphere, Condition and Duties, of Woman*, ed. Arthur B. Fuller (Boston: John P. Jewett & Company, 1855).

4. *Memoirs of Margaret Fuller Ossoli*, ed. Ralph Waldo Emerson, William Henry Channing, and James Freeman Clarke (Boston: Phillips, Sampson and Company, 1852).

5. Ralph L. Rusk, *The Life of Ralph Waldo Emerson* (New York: Charles Scribner's Sons, 1949), p. 378.

6. Fuller Papers and Manuscripts, Houghton Library, Harvard University. Reprinted by permission of the Houghton Library.

7. *Margaret Fuller: American Romantic: A Selection from her Writings and Correspondence*, ed. Perry Miller (1963; rpt., Ithaca, N.Y.: Cornell Paperbacks, 1970), p. 317.

8. Joseph Jay Deiss, *The Roman Years of Margaret Fuller* (New York: Thomas Y. Crowell Company, 1969), p. viii.

9. For interesting insights, see the notebook Emerson kept while editing *Memoirs: The Journals and Miscellaneous Notebooks of Ralph Waldo Emerson*, ed. William H. Gilman et al. (Cambridge: Harvard University Press, 1975), 11:445–509. Emerson observed: "The unlooked for trait in all these journals to me is the Woman, poor woman: they are all hysterical. She is bewailing her virginity and languishing for a husband" (p. 500).

10. The friend was Elizabeth Hoar. The men he mentioned in his journal are Mickiewicz, Mazzini, and Ossoli who "prosecuted his suit against all denial." *Journals of Emerson*, 11:503.

11. Quotations from *Memoirs*, 1:234, 202, 229.

12. Ibid., pp. 281–283.

13. Ibid., p. 279.

14. *Journals of Emerson*, 11:470–471.

15. *Memoirs*, 1:324.

16. Ibid., p. 78.

17. Ibid., p. 94.

18. See Derek Colville, "The Transcendental Friends: Clarke and Margaret Fuller," *New England Quarterly* 30 (September 1957): 378–382, for a concise analysis of the differences in their personalities and the high caliber of friendship Fuller insisted upon.

19. *Memoirs*, 1:61, 2:9.

20. Ibid., 2:156–163.

21. See Helene G. Baer, *The Heart Is Like Heaven: The Life of Lydia Maria Child* (Philadelphia: University of Pennsylvania Press, 1964), pp. 181–186. Helene G. Baer contends that Mrs. Greeley suspected that her husband had

fallen in love with his lady reporter. After Margaret moved out of the Greeley home, her visits to the estate became infrequent due to Mary Greeley's jealousy, as "Margaret had captured the heart of the Greeleys' son Pickie, as well as his father's."

22. *Memoirs*, 1:91–92.

23. Carl F. Strauch, "Hatred's Swift Repulsions: Emerson, Margaret Fuller, and Others," *Studies in Romanticism* 7 (Winter 1968): 65–103.

24. *Journals of Emerson*, 7:400.

25. *Memoirs*, 1:288, 230.

26. For an analysis of Emerson's feelings, see "The Ambivalence of Ralph Waldo Emerson towards Margaret Fuller," *Thoreau Journal Quarterly* 10 (July 1978): 26–36.

27. *Journals of Emerson*, 11:258.

28. See *The Correspondence of Emerson and Carlyle*, ed. Joseph Slater (New York: Columbia University Press, 1964), p. 462. In a letter dated August 5, 1850, Emerson wrote: "You will have heard our sad news of Margaret Fuller Marchesa Ossoli. She was drowned with her husband and child on the wreck of the ship Elizabeth on the 19 July, at 3 in the P.M. after sitting all day, from morning, in plain sight of the shore of Long Island, New York.—I doubt you never saw in her what was inestimable here. But she died in happy hour for herself. Her health was much exhausted. Her marriage would have taken her away from us all, and there was a subsistence yet to be secured, and diminished powers, and old age."

29. Fuller understood Emerson's feelings. In a letter to her sister Ellen, on December 11, 1849, she wrote: "About Ossoli, I do not like to say much, as he is an exceedingly delicate person. . . . I expect to many of my friends, Mr. Emerson for one ["Mr. Emerson" crossed out by an editor] he will be nothing and they will not understand that I should have life in common with him." Fuller MSS, 9:171. Reprinted by permission of Houghton Library.

30. Letter to Margaret Fuller, July 11, 1843, *The Letters of Ralph Waldo Emerson*, ed. Ralph L. Rusk (New York: Columbia University Press, 1939), 3:183.

31. Emerson to Fuller, August 30, 1844, in ibid, vol. 3.

32. *Memoirs*, 1:321–322.

33. Study of Emerson's life and journals indicates that he was much less willing to accept female emancipation than many other transcendentalists were. For example, he wrote, women "exist to take care of men." He could recognize the problems of ordinary women as opposed to the ideal: "what hundreds of extremely ordinary, paltry, hopeless women I see, whose plight is piteous to think of." *Journals of Emerson*, 11:234, 444.

34. *Memoirs*, 2:138–144.

35. Ibid., pp. 152–158.

36. See Joel Myerson, *Margaret Fuller: An Annotated Secondary Bibliography* (New York: Burt Franklin & Company, 1977), for some of the comments. He includes at least forty-six reviews.

37. Ironically, as an old man, Emerson modified his opinion of Fuller as a writer. Alcott recorded in his March 8, 1877, journal that Emerson had been rereading Fuller's letters. Emerson said they were "more brilliant and remarkable than he knew till his late readings." *The Journals of Bronson Alcott*, ed. Odell Shepard (Boston: Little, Brown, 1938), p. 474.

38. Helen Neill McMaster, "Margaret Fuller as a Literary Critic," *University of Buffalo Studies* 7 (December 1928): 38.

39. *Memoirs*, 1:202–203.

40. Richard Frederick Fuller, "The Younger Generation in 1840 from the Diary of a New England Boy," *Atlantic Monthly Magazine* 136 (August 1925): 216–224.

41. *The Works of Edgar Allen Poe*, ed. Edmund Clarence Stedman and George Edward Woodberry (New York: The Colonial Company, Limited, 1895), 8:83–85. Poe's emphasis.

42. Madeleine B. Stern, *The Life of Margaret Fuller* (New York: Dutton, 1942), pp. 368–370.

43. *Letters of Emerson*, 3:183.

44. Henry David Thoreau, *A Week on the Concord and Merrimack Rivers, The Writings of Henry David Thoreau* (Boston: Houghton Mifflin, 1892), 1:296. For an account of the Thoreau-Fuller interaction, see "Henry David Thoreau and Margaret Fuller," *Thoreau Journal Quarterly* 8 (October 1976).

45. Foreword by Perry Miller to *Margaret Fuller: American Romantic*, p. ix.

46. Strangely enough, if Fuller appeared too "masculine" to Hawthorne, a glimpse of an early Hawthorne short story, "The Gentle Boy," led her to believe that it had been written by a woman: "There's a very fine woman's contribution in the last issue of *The Token*. It's called 'The Gentle Boy.' I'm sure it's by a woman, although there's no signature." Stern, *Life of Fuller*, p. 67.

47. Ironically, Fuller thought Hawthorne had made a mistake about her sex when her first article was published on November 27, 1834, in the *Boston Daily Advertiser*. Three days after her work appeared, she received a letter from Salem, signed "H," supporting Bancroft's position. Because her piece had been signed with the letter, "J," her critic, she reported, "detected some ignorance in me and seemed to consider me an elderly gentleman yet said I wrote 'with ability.' I consider the affair highly flattering and beg you

to furnish it for my memoirs when I am dead." She guessed the identity of the writer from Salem as Hawthorne, whom at the time she had never met. Ibid., pp. 82–83. (Myerson's *Secondary Bibliography* does not identify the author of the letter who refuted her defense of Brutus.)

48. *Autobiography of Brook Farm*, ed. Henry W. Sams (Englewood Cliffs, N.J.: Prentice-Hall, 1958), pp. 13–14.

49. Julian Hawthorne, *Nathaniel Hawthorne and His Wife: A Biography* (1884; rpt., Michigan: Scholarly Press, 1968), 1:255–256.

50. Ibid., pp. 259–261.

51. Nathaniel Hawthorne, *The Blithedale Romance*, introduction by Arlin Turner (New York: Norton, 1958), p. 43. All subsequent quotations are from this edition. Turner argues there are more differences than similarities between Fuller and Zenobia.

52. *Memoirs*, 1:235.

53. Fuller sent the Hawthornes a copy when it was published. To their letter of acknowledgment, she replied "that at the moment she was weary of discussing it." Mason Wade, *Margaret Fuller: Whetstone of Genius* (New York: Viking Press, 1940), p. 112.

54. Horace Greeley, *Recollections of a Busy Life* (New York: J. B. Ford, 1868), p. 179.

55. Katharine Anthony, in her psychological biography, *Margaret Fuller* (New York: Harcourt, 1920), p. 93, explains Hawthorne's hostility: "No doubt he received the same sort of emotional satisfaction from vilifying her that his near ancestor had received from whipping a witch through the streets of Salem."

56. Oliver Wendell Holmes, "Cinders from the Ashes," *Atlantic Monthly* 23 (January 1869): 116–117.

57. *Memoirs*, 2:35–36.

58. Oliver Wendell Holmes, *Elsie Venner-A Romance of Destiny*, 32d ed. (Boston: Houghton Mifflin, 1887), pp. 130-131.

59. Clarence P. Oberndorf, *The Psychiatric Novels of Oliver Wendell Holmes* (New York: Columbia University Press, 1943), p. 222n. Dr. Oberndorf's comments still reflect dislike of Fuller as well as a bias against women who wish to excel.

60. Henry James, *The Bostonians*, introduction by Philip Rahv (New York: Dial Press, 1945), p. 15. Rahv argues that the cause of feminism is not the vital center of the book but rather is a catchall for the excesses and distortions James satirizes. The character Miss Birdseye is identified as a picture of the venerable Elizabeth Peabody.

61. Henry James, *William Whetmore Story and His Friends* (1903; rpt., New York: Grove Press, 1957), 1:127–128.

62. Ibid., pp. 103–105.

63. Sarah Josepha Hale, *Woman's Record; or, Sketches of All Distinguished Women from the Creation to A.D. 1854* (1855; rpt., New York: Source Book Press, 1970), p. 667.

64. Margaret Fuller Ossoli, *At Home and Abroad, or Things and Thoughts in America and Europe*, ed. Arthur B. Fuller (1856; rpt., Port Washington, N.Y.: Kennikat Press, 1971), preface.

65. Julia Ward Howe, *Margaret Fuller* (1883; rpt., Boston: Little, Brown, 1905), pp. 151–153.

66. *Love-Letters of Margaret Fuller, 1845–1846*, with an introduction by Julia Ward Howe (1903; rpt., New York: Greenwood Press, 1969), pp. v–xii passim.

67. Thomas Wentworth Higginson, *Margaret Fuller Ossoli* (1884; rpt., Boston: Houghton Mifflin, 1887), pp. 2–5, 287–293.

68. For more details, see the biography of this remarkable man by Howard N. Meyer, *Colonel of the Black Regiment* (New York: Norton, 1967).

69. *American Literary Criticism*, ed. William Morton Payne (1904; rpt., Freeport, N.Y.: Books for Libraries Press, 1968), p. 22.

70. Margaret Bell, *Margaret Fuller* (New York: Charles Boni Paper Books, 1930), p. 14.

71. *Cambridge History of American Literature* (New York: G. P. Putnam's, 1917), 1:342.

72. Arthur Hobson Quinn, "The Establishment of National Literature," in *The Literature of the American People* (New York: Appleton-Century-Crofts, 1957), p. 274.

73. Perry Miller, "I Find No Intellect Comparable to My Own," *American Heritage* 8 (February 1957): 99.

74. Joel Myerson, "Margaret Fuller: An Exhibition from the Collection of Joel L. Myerson" (Columbia: University of South Carolina, 1973), finds this picture is from Mrs. Newton Crosland's *Memorable Women* (Boston: Ticknor, Reed, and Fields, 1854).

75. *Margaret Fuller: American Romantic*, ed. Perry Miller, pp. xvii, 135, xiii.

76. Elizabeth Cady Stanton, Susan B. Anthony, and Matilda Joslyn Gage, eds., *History of Woman Suffrage* (New York: Fowler & Wells, 1881–1887), 2:266. The editors dedicated *History* to Margaret Fuller as well as to other pioneer feminists with the inscription that their "earnest lives and fearless words, in demanding political rights for women, have been, in the preparation of these pages, a constant inspiration."

77. *At Home and Abroad*, letter to her sister, June 19, 1849, p. 437.

78. Deiss, *Roman Years*, pp. 67–70, 291–292. See also his "Humanity,

Said Edgar Allen Poe, Is Divided into Men, Women, and Margaret Fuller,"
*American Heritage* 23 (August 1972): 43–47, 94–97.

79. Glendy Culligan, book review, *Saturday Review*, 52 (December 20,
1969): 27, 73.

# Chapter 2  Early radical thought

The history of women's rights saw its first major study in 1792 with the publication of Mary Wollstonecraft's *A Vindication of the Rights of Woman*. This germinal work covered much of the same material as its American counterpart, *Woman in the Nineteenth Century*, but the tempers of the two works differed. *A Vindication of the Rights of Woman* was a rational yet heated defense of women's rights, while *Woman in the Nineteenth Century* was a transcendentalist and erudite statement.

Novelist George Eliot in 1855 compared the two works, remarking that both share in strong understanding and important ideas. Just five years after Fuller's death, Eliot observed that her book had already been "unduly thrust into the background by less comprehensive and candid productions on the same subject." As for Wollstonecraft's book, Eliot found a "vague prejudice" among people who had not read it, but it was "eminently serious, severely moral, and withal rather heavy." Editions were hard to locate because none had been issued since 1796. Although Eliot did not make a comprehensive comparison, she found Fuller more literary and Wollstonecraft writing under the pressure of other motives. She was especially impressed with the idea that both feminists shared: men pay a heavy price for their reluctance to encourage self-help in women because their "doll-Madonna" is fit for nothing.[1]

Wollstonecraft's Enlightenment theories were introduced to Fuller as a young child by her father. When only a junior at Harvard, Timothy Fuller read Wollstonecraft's feminist work and at that time conceived the idea of rigorously educating a daughter, yet to be born, according to principles advocated by Wollstonecraft. In later years Fuller wrote in her autobiographical memoir how her father had instructed her as a child: "A Queen Anne's man, he hoped to make me heir of all he knew." She recounted that as a small child she had to recite to him every night what she had learned during the day. When she started Latin at age six, her impatient father expected her to translate for him "without breaks or hesitation." She was not allowed to express her ideas unless she could give a reason for them or make a statement "unless sure of particulars." She later complained that this intense education kept her in a state of anxiety, causing her insomnia and nightmares because her father did not understand the importance of the emotions—of "imagination and feeling."[2] Nevertheless, her later erudition and well-reasoned writing were a testimony to the efficacy of her father's tutoring. *A Vindication of the Rights of Woman* stressed the necessity of a good and disciplined education for girls similar to that for boys, but it did not specifically advocate as demanding a program as Timothy Fuller's.

Better education for girls was the key factor to improve the lot of women that Wollstonecraft promulgated in *Vindication*, whereas in *Woman*, although Fuller advocated Wollstonecraft's idea of broader and more practical educational opportunities for girls, her panacea was spiritual self-perfection. As a generalization, it could be postulated that despite the fact that Wollstonecraft and Fuller started from different philosophical premises, many of their particular solutions to problems confronting women were similar.[3] Philosophically, Wollstonecraft buttressed her position with arguments derived from natural rights, whereas Fuller's basic premise was in accord with transcendentalist concepts of growth. Wollstonecraft subscribed to Locke's theory that man was the product of his environment, and Fuller concurred in the transcendental view that the individual must make his own world. The overall tone of *Vindication* is one of disillusion and indignation; that of *Woman* is one of expectation and optimism.

The tone of each woman's treatise reflects the immediate circumstances that caused her to write it. Wollstonecraft was writing in anger, Fuller in hope. Subconsciously, no doubt, each woman had been preparing to write her protest all of her life, but the event that prompted Wollstonecraft to write hers was her indignation with the plan of education for the new French constitution outlined by M. Talleyrand-Perigord, to whom she dedicated her work. Abandoning some of the egalitarian principles of the French Revolution, Talleyrand-Perigord proposed that girls be educated in the schools with boys only until age eight. Thereafter the girls would be expected to stay home and learn domestic duties.[4] Wollstonecraft's immediate impetus to write *Vindication* was her concern with the proper education for girls, while Fuller's was to expand her dialogue essay, "The Great Lawsuit:—Man *versus* Men; Woman *versus* Women," which had originally been published in the *Dial*. Hence *Woman* expressed the transcendental optimism that permeated much of the writing in the *Dial* and was in certain respects broader in its scope than *Vindication* was.

In order to understand *A Vindication of the Rights of Woman* (1792), it is important to keep in mind that it had been preceded by Wollstonecraft's publication of *A Vindication of the Rights of Men* (1790), also written in indignant haste in response to an opinion with which Wollstonecraft disagreed. On this occasion she attacked the distinguished Whig Edmund Burke for his stand in *Reflections on the Revolution in France*. "Historically and thematically" *A Vindication of the Rights of Men* is an "introduction to *A Vindication of the Rights of Woman*" because it develops the abstract principles that Wollstonecraft first used to defend the rights of men in opposition to Burke's conservative position.[5] Hence, as scholars have observed, Wollstonecraft's basic position in both books was that of natural rights. The way that she developed the idea in *A Vindication of the Rights of Woman* was to meet the issue squarely: if women are indeed human beings—and not overgrown children or brute animals—then their natural rights must not be denied them. The inherent rights of men have no sexual basis, so she argued: "In short, in whatever light I view the subject, reason and experience convince me that the only method of leading women to fulfil their peculiar duties, is to free them from all restraint by allowing them to participate the inherent rights of mankind" (p. 261). Fuller also accepted this concept—"All

men are born free and equal"—as a "golden certainty." She concluded with the optimistic belief that application of this law to every
member of society was inevitable.[6]

The difference between the works is that Fuller acknowledged
natural rights as accepted theory, whereas Wollstonecraft emphasized them as a major basis for her argument. Hence the tone and
main thrust of their arguments differed. Although generally assum-
ing different philosophic stances to promulgate their theses, both
feminists used many of the same analogies to illustrate society's
unfair treatment of women. For example, Wollstonecraft repeatedly
compared a woman's lot to the life of a slave—"Why do they expect
virtue from a slave?" (p. 86)—and the life of a fashionable lady to life
in a seraglio. Later both slavery and the seraglio were favorite
comparisons of Fuller, and of other feminists too. Thus, she wrote
in *Woman:* "In the country of Lady Russell, the custom of English
peeresses, of selling their daughters to the highest bidder, is made
the theme and jest of fashionable novels by unthinking children who
would stare at the idea of sending them to a Turkish slave-dealer,
though the circumstances of the bargain are there less degrading" (p.
139). However, Wollstonecraft used some analogies apparently too
strong for Fuller to adopt, as when she compared the conduct
expected of women to dogs—"a spaniel-like affection . . . smiling
under the lash at which it dare not snarl" (p. 68)—to cats—"a kind of
cattish affection which leads a wife to purr about her husband as she
would about any man who fed and caressed her" (p. 260)—and to
birds, an analogy that may have inspired later song writers who used
the gilded-cage image—"Confined then in cages like the feathered
race, they have nothing to do but to plume themselves, and stalk
with mock majesty from perch to perch" (p. 98). At times sarcastic—"insipid softness, varnished over with the name of gentleness" (p. 59)—Wollstonecraft was often more trenchant than
Fuller. Nevertheless, both were scornful of fashionable ladies, but
Wollstonecraft even went so far as to declare in her introduction that
her instruction was not applicable to ladies and was directed to the
middle class "because they appear to be in the most natural state" (p.
33). A recurrent theme throughout her polemic was a denunciation
of the weak, artificial ladies who corrupted all of society, and Fuller
too echoed this thought when she complained of ladies who misused

their talents: "I saw their eyes restlessly courting attention" (p. 145). She even took the position that ladies who misused their advantages were on a morally lower scale than prostitutes—"the women of the prison stood fairest . . . because they had misused less light" (p. 146)—and she also blamed the ladies for the plight of the prostitutes—"Now I ask you, my sisters, if the women at the fashionable house be not answerable for those women being in prison?" (p. 146). What seems evident from an examination of both works is that Wollstonecraft and Fuller believed (as contemporary feminists do) that social concepts of the role expected of a lady hindered her moral growth and development as a person.

Fuller also expressed an idea, reiterated throughout *Vindication*, that the chief drawback in a woman's education was that she was taught she "was created for man" (p. 59). She repeated this thought:  "not one man, in the million, shall I say? no, not in the hundred million, can rise above the belief that Woman was made *for Man*" (p. 36). Because this view prevailed in society, it followed logically that the main focus of a girl's education was how to make herself pleasing to men. According to Wollstonecraft, in order to learn "how to get a man," girls were educated in principles that lead "to a system of cunning and lasciviousness" (p. 129). The moral price for this type of dissimulation was high; it rendered "women pleasing at the expense of every solid virtue" (p. 53). Fuller expressed a similar idea: "But it was power which hurt alike them and those against whom they made use of the arms of the servile,—cunning, blandishment, and unreasonable emotion" (p. 172).

Furthermore, Wollstonecraft argued that instead of fostering independence in a girl, as education should, this system of education exalted a woman's weakness into a virtue. She developed this point at some length, attacking and quoting from authors who advocated this type of education for girls—writers as obscure as Dr. James Fordyce (*Sermons to Young Women*) and Dr. John Gregory (*Father's Legacy to His Daughters*) and as notable as Jean Jacques Rousseau (*Emile*). Despite the fact that some of Wollstonecraft's philosophic ideas of natural goodness and perfectibility were derived from Rousseau, his ideas about the education of girls were those with which Wollstonecraft took strong issue. She disagreed with his theories of education in *Emile* because Sophia's primary role was to be pleasing to her master. Wollstonecraft believed that Rousseau chose to degrade women to justify his weakness in his affection for "that fool Theresa" (p. 259). Instead of educating girls to be pleasing to men, Wollstonecraft wrote, it would be better to consider "women in the grand light of human creatures, who, in common with men, are placed on this earth to unfold their faculties" (p. 33). Although Fuller did not attack "authorities" as boldly as Wollstonecraft did, she used the transcendental concept of individual growth as a key point in her book.

Both women also took an unorthodox view of Christianity. Wollstonecraft asserted that the biblical account of the fall of man was not literally true (p. 130), and Fuller stated that Christianity has made no improvement in the condition of woman (p. 48).

The central issue related to the dilemmas facing women was the question of marriage. Wollstonecraft's discussion of marriage raised many key problems confronting women, especially ambitious women. One of her main points—frequently dealt with by subsequent feminist writers—was that the only way a woman could rise in the world was to marry advantageously so that in effect many wives were "legal prostitutes" (p. 104). She, of course, would like to give them other avenues for advancement. Furthermore, Wollstonecraft discussed the problems of prostitutes in a sympathetic way, later emulated by the bolder feminists, including Fuller. If, then, Wollstonecraft did not want a woman to be a legal or common prostitute, when did she find marriage most justified? In *Vindication* she took the unsentimental view that "love, from its very nature, must be transitory" (p. 63). Because either friendship, "the most holy band of society," or indifference succeeds love, she advocated friendship between husband and wife as a better bond than sexual passion. This is one of the major points with which her view is at variance with Fuller's, who recognized that friendship and intellectual companionship between husband and wife are of value but who held that the highest type of marriage derives from common religious goals. Fuller did not take it for granted that love has to die with marriage, so her outlook might be characterized as idealistic, whereas Wollstonecraft's could be categorized as realistic or rational.

Ultimately both writers thought that expanded opportunities for women would also benefit men. In *Vindication* Wollstonecraft wrote that the "two sexes mutually corrupt and improve each other" (p. 210). She again embellished this point after reiterating her appeal to a belief in the inherent rights of mankind, with vivid imagery: "Let men take their choice, man and woman were made for each other, though not to become one being; and if they will not improve women, they will deprave them!" (p. 261). Fuller modified Wollstonecraft's idea when taking the stand that men and women have a common being: "But yet—his habits and his will corrupted by the past—he did not clearly see that Woman was half himself; that her interests were identical with his; and that, by the law of their common being, he could never reach his true proportions while she remained in any wise shorn of hers" (p. 171). Thus Fuller argued a major thesis: man cannot realize his true potential unless woman can realize hers. She opened her work with the epigraphs that set forth this thesis: "Frailty, thy name is WOMAN" and "The Earth waits for her Queen." Then she repeated the epigraphs but reversed the sex, changing "woman" to "man" and "Queen" to "King," making it clear that her admonitions applied to both sexes. In her peroration, she again alluded to her epigraphs, making the inter-dependence of the sexes clear: "On himself came the punishment. He educated Woman more as a servant than a daughter, and found himself a king without a queen" (p. 170). And when speaking of the contempt people feel for the unmarried, Fuller was careful to praise the contributions made both by old maids and old bachelors (pp. 96–97).[7]

Another point Wollstonecraft raised to support her idea that it was in the interest of men to encourage independence in their wives concerns a mother's influence on her children (p. 263). Fuller, like Wollstonecraft, demonstrated that weak women make poor mothers: "The children of this unequal union showed unequal natures, and, more and more, men seemed sons of the handmaid, rather than princess" (p. 170). Whether she was discussing woman as wife, mother, spinster, or prostitute, Fuller contended that it was in the best interest of man to give woman equal rights.

Because these theoreticians would have liked to see women able to be independent of men, they advocated expanded employment opportunities for women. Wollstonecraft suggested they could engage in business, practice as physicians, regulate a farm, or manage a shop (pp. 222–223); Fuller called for a greater range of occupations. In this discussion Fuller gave her sensational carte blanche: "But if you ask me what offices they may fill, I reply—any. I do not care what case you put; let them be sea-captains, if you will" (p. 174). In this case, Fuller was more radical than Wollstonecraft because she left the field of employment open.

Despite the fact that these two early feminists had much in common and that Margaret Fuller was greatly indebted to Mary Wollstonecraft for her synthesis of many ideas, it is important to keep in mind that Wollstonecraft was a product of the Enlightenment and Fuller of transcendentalism. Although Wollstonecraft acknowledged the existence of God, she said that religion must be founded on reason (p. 176). Her panacea for the problems besetting mankind was education, whereas Fuller's solution was religion. Fuller used, as parenthetical to the law of right, the law of growth that speaks from within (pp. 176–177).

The considerable difference in attitude between the two books begins with the significance of the titles. Mary Wollstonecraft, boldly asserting a woman's rights, was writing a true vindication engendered by a sense of indignation of one who had held high hopes for the social changes of the French Revolution, only to find that the educational conditions of girls were not going to improve after all. Hers was the outraged voice of the disappointed idealist, cheated of her dreams, who blamed men for using their reason to justify their prejudices. Margaret Fuller expressed the optimism of the transcendentalists as she admonished women to stand alone and to stick to their principles: "If principles could be established, particulars would adjust themselves aright" (p. 33). At times, Wollstonecraft was sarcastic: "The common source of consolation is, that such women [rational conversationalists] seldom get husbands" (p. 261). Both women, however, mentioned taboo subjects, such as abortions (*Vindication*, p. 209) and pregnant slaves working in the fields (*Woman*, p. 35), but Wollstonecraft was blunter and more caustic; Fuller more often subtly veiled her ideas in classical allusions and irony.

At first glance, *Vindication* seems better organized than *Woman*. It provides a clear statement of purpose in the introduction, but as the book proceeds, it appears redundant. Moreover, Wollstonecraft's sentences and paragraphs follow more formal rhetorical structure, while Fuller's sentence and paragraph patterns are sometimes in the form of dialogues, sometimes exclamations; at other times they follow rhetorical principles of inductive or deductive logic.[8] A hundred pages longer than *Woman*, however, *Vindication* tends to be repetitive and could have been shortened without weakening its message. *Woman*, rich with literary allusions from Western civilization, is more psychologically complex. Whether from the pressure of Wollstonecraft's repetition or Fuller's plethora of illustrations, both treatises occasionally create the effect of verbosity.

Since Margaret Fuller was so indebted to *Vindication* as the prototype of feminist protest literature, why does she equate Mary Wollstonecraft with George Sand and say her existence, more than anything she wrote, proved the need for a reinterpretation of woman's rights? In the same paragraph she praised William Godwin's defense of his wife's cause, and later praised his marriage to the "calumniated authoress" as a sign of a new era (pp. 75, 77). Fuller probably felt it necessary to take this attitude because Wollstonecraft had become a symbol of the despised Jacobinism, and was attacked after her death as a wanton, a prostitute. Ironically enough, Godwin himself made it possible for critics to attack his wife's morality. In *Memoirs*, a kind of memorial biography, he candidly gave details of her love affair with Gilbert Imlay, even going so far as to publish the love letters Mary had written to Imlay. Godwin also revealed other unhappy aspects of his wife's life, such as her attempts at suicide. Consequently, she was either castigated by the Tory press or ignored in books dealing with female authors.[9] Fuller must, therefore, have felt the need to apologize for Wollstonecraft's unconventional life by explaining that she had become an outlaw because her bonds were too narrow, rather than directly giving her credit for what she had written. Instead, Godwin received credit for marrying and being loyal to a "calumniated" woman.

Although Fuller did not give as much recognition to Mary Wollstonecraft as she deserved, she did adapt many of her ideas and then reshaped them in the transcendental metaphor.

Fuller wrote a review of two novels that depicted the rational Enlightenment heroine educated according to Mary Wollstonecraft's theory, *Ormond* and *Wieland* by Charles Brockden-Brown. In the *New York Tribune*, July 21, 1846, a year and a half after *Woman* was published, she said: "We rejoice to see these reprints of Brown's novels as we have long been ashamed that one who ought to be the pride of the country, and who is, in the higher qualities of the mind, so far in advance of our other novelists, should have become almost inaccessible to the public." Furthermore, in her essay, "American Literature," also written in 1846, she wrote:

> We see we have omitted honoured names in this essay. We have not spoken of Brown, as a novelist by far our first in point of genius and instruction as to the soul of things. Yet his works have fallen almost out of print. It is their dark, deep gloom that prevents their being popular, for their very beauties are grave and sad. But we see that *Ormond* is being republished at this moment.[10]

In both of these comments she implied that she had been familiar with Brown's novels for some time (possibly since the 1827 edition). It is therefore possible to infer that Brown's sensible heroines who stubbornly adhered to their convictions may have given encouragement to Fuller in her search for her own identity. She further observed in her review that Brown was a "prophet . . . of a better era," because "he has usually placed this thinking, royal mind in the body of a woman." She continued with the viewpoint first espoused  by Mary Wollstonecraft that the "term *feminine* is not a synonym for *weak.*" She elaborated on this point with more specific references to the resourcefulness and courage of Brown's heroines, Clara Wieland and Constantia Dudley.

If, therefore, it is true that Brown's novels are "the testing grounds of ideas," it can be postulated that his *Ormond* concerns not only the value of reason as a rule of life, but also the problems faced by a young and beautiful woman who must make her way in the world.[11] *Ormond* examines limited employment opportunities for women as well as questions of matrimony. The villain, Ormond, does not believe in marriage as an institution. Constantia Dudley, on the other hand, takes a serious approach to marriage. As a young woman, she refuses to marry impetuously, despite the fact that she is attracted to her suitor. Her judgment proves to be correct when the young man deserts her after her father loses his fortune. Even when she and her blind father are poverty-stricken, she refuses an offer of marriage by a middle-aged wealthy merchant because of his limited intelligence. Hence Constantia prefers freedom with poverty to security with a man she does not respect. In addition, she urges Ormond to marry the girl who has been his mistress. As Fuller wrote, it does seem evident that Brown has put the "thinking mind" in the body of a woman.

Another of Brown's works influenced by Enlightenment reasoning deals directly with the subject of woman's rights. Fuller may never have heard of this early American publication, *Alcuin*. Its circulation was limited at the time of the publication of Parts I and II in 1798, and the rest of the book with its visionary utopia was not published until 1815 as a part of William Dunlap's biography of Brown. Many of Brown's arguments in *Alcuin* seem to be derived from Mary Wollstonecraft's *A Vindication of the Rights of Woman;* for example, he used "dog," analogous to her "spaniel," when characterizing the devotion expected of a wife to her husband.[12] Since *Alcuin* is in dialogue form, however, it is interesting to speculate that Fuller might have seen it and been encouraged to use this device in "The Great Lawsuit." This is mere speculation, however, because dialogues were a popular literary device at the time, as illustrated by the popularity of Landor's imaginary conversations. Also, the dialogue form is an excellent way for a writer to debate ideas without committing himself. *Alcuin* is inconclusive.[13]

Although Fuller did not acknowledge either Charles Brockden Brown or Mary Wollstonecraft as sources, in *Woman* she did credit Charles Fourier for his ideas. In addition to Fourier's socialist theory, his corollary ideas concerning diverse employment, liberty of law, and the importance of the emotions were influential in Fuller's thinking. She read all of her sources with a questing spirit for material she could use to reinforce her position that opportunities for women should be expanded. Fourier's revolutionary way of looking at the world—that one must doubt all received opinions—helped Fuller to see that customs and attitudes could be changed. She did not accept all of his ideas but acknowledged his ability to inspire: "He has filled one department of instruction for the new era, and the harmony in action, and freedom for individual

growth, he hopes, shall exist; and, if the methods he proposes should
not prove the true ones, yet his fair propositions shall give many
hints, and make room for the inspiration needed, for such" (pp.
123–24). She read Fourier's *Le Nouveau monde industriel et sociétaire*
just prior to writing her revised version of "The Great Lawsuit," so
it was fresh in her memory. However, she declined to join Brook
Farm, which was based on Fourier's ideas, although she was well
acquainted with Sophia and George Ripley. Her decision was probably due to her financial problems, and her dislike of farm life at her
father's farm in Groton, as well as her belief that adequate plans had
not been made for the experiment. She observed in a letter to
William Henry Channing:

> In town I saw the Ripleys. Mr. R. more and more wrapt in his
> new project. He is too sanguine, and does not take time to let
> things ripen in his mind; yet his aim is worthy, and with his
> courage and clear mind his experiment will not, I think, to him
> at least, be a failure. I will not throw any cold water, yet I
> would wish him the aid of some equal and faithful friend in the
> beginning, the rather that his own mind, though that of a
> captain, is not that of a conqueror.[14]

Nevertheless, she visited Brook Farm and confided to her journal
other observations:

> My hopes might lead to Association, too,—an association, if
> not of efforts, yet of destinies. In such an one I live with several
> already, feeling that each one, by acting out his own, casts
> light upon a mutual destiny, and illustrates the thought of a
> master mind. It is a constellation, not a phalanx, to which I
> would belong.

By her preference for the word *constellation* to that of Fourier's
*phalanx*, she seemed to be suggesting that the collective life was not
exalted enough for her. Also it is worth noting that, writing after a
visit there, she realistically recognized Brook Farm for what it
was—an experiment: "Why bind oneself to a central or any doctrine? How much nobler stands a man entirely unpledged, un-
bound! Association may be the great experiment of the age, still it is

only an experiment. It is not worth while to lay such stress on it; let us try it, induce others to try it,—that is enough."[15] If, then, Fuller declined to join the Brook Farm communal experiment, supposedly following Fourier's doctrines under the aegis of Arthur Brisbane and the Ripleys, it seems reasonable to conclude that she did not expect a collective farm to do much more for women's rights than provide the atmosphere in which discussion could take place.

The associationists at Brook Farm did not follow Fourier's ideas precisely as set forth in his writings, to which they had access. They had neither enough people to form a trial phalanx nor enough money to build a model phalanstery. Although Fourier believed that many housewives and children were parasites, the Brook Farm commune did not practice the kind of sex equality that he advocated: "The distribution of tasks must assure each man, woman, or child the right to work or the right to take part at any time in any kind of work for which he or she is qualified."[16] Hawthorne complained about having to load twenty or thirty carts of manure, but no women at Brook Farm were known to do this task.[17] Fuller had praised Fourier in *Woman* for his attitude toward the equality of men and women: "He, too, places Woman on an entire equality with Man, and wishes to give to one as to the other that independence which must result from intellectual and practical development" (p. 124). But what she had derived from the socialists and other visionary thinkers so numerous at the time, as well as the people at Brook Farm, was theoretical reinforcement of the idea that the world was not static. If the Brook Farm experiment did not work, there were other experiments in living to try.

In *Woman* she classified Charles Fourier with Emanuel Swedenborg and Johann Wolfgang von Goethe as "the prophets of the coming age." She thought that the positions of Swedenborg and Fourier were somewhat similar, with Fourier expressing outwardly the secret springs that Swedenborg had divined. Initially she described Goethe's ideas as the opposite of Fourier's, citing Goethe's preoccupation with the individual and Fourier's with institutions, but she finally noted that they were marching in the same army. She perceived a great similarity between Goethe's and Fourier's hopes and the ends that were reached by different roads. Furthermore, she applauded Swedenborg's view of men and women as sharing an "angelic ministry" and Fourier's advocacy of self-help for women (pp. 122–130).

Later, in a letter from Europe, she added that Fourier's doctrines were an attempt at the practical application "of the precepts of Christ." It is obvious that she considered Fourier's views of a high order, although she complained that he made the soul a result of the body's health rather than the body as the "clothing of the soul."[18] Therefore, it seems worthwhile to examine Fourier's works that influenced her writing of *Woman*. Although *Le Nouveau monde amoureux* had not been published during her or Fourier's lifetimes, there is enough of his passional attraction theory in his other works to make it clear that he believed the thwarting of the instinctive life was a cause of human misery.[19] This idea probably inspired Fuller to write of Fourier as the "apostle of the new order, of the social fabric that is to rise from love, and supersede the old that was based on strife" (p. 123). However, instead of accepting his suggested fuller sex life for both men and women, she called for higher standards of chastity for both sexes. Nor did she express his opposition to monogamy, which he thought enslaved both sexes, particularly women. Her chief interests were in his theory of attractive industry, his attitude toward women, and his basic premise that all received opinions must be approached with *l'écart absolu*. Fourier's attack was on Western society itself: "Such is the illusion of progress in which our old civilization glories as it hastens toward decrepitude. Societies like individuals go to their ruin when they fall into debt and sell themselves to the usurer. This is the fact of our time; we are moving from one loan to another."[20] As a general proposition, he considered a society's attitude toward the liberty of women as a barometer of social progress. He used different societies' treatment of women as a pivotal criterion for evaluating them from the primitive and savage ages to the civilization of his own day, which he felt would soon be supplanted. No doubt Fourier's historical survey gave impetus to Fuller's careful scrutiny of contemporary attitudes toward the status of women. In her peroration, she reflected and refined some of his concepts of society's need for harmony, as well as his prophecy that a new era was dawning.

She recommended Fourier's program of attractive industry when she asked that men give women "a much greater range of occupation than they have" (p. 174). Since Fourier's work forces were composed of men and women doing work usually reserved for one or the other sex (for example, "nurse men" for small children as well as "nurse women"), he must have encouraged Fuller's idea that other avenues of employment besides needlework, teaching, and housework should be opened to women. Fourier's theory of attractive industry shows his psychological acumen because he believed that work should be a source of satisfaction to workers; moreover, people doing work they loathe do not perform it efficiently. His proposed motivation is suggestive of modern behavioral modification psychology, for he advocated reinforcement in food, honor, and praise by peers and community for work well done. He devised his utopian society in exhaustive detail, solving the problem of how to get loathsome work done, such as removing manure and garbage. This was no easy task in his libertarian world of both life and work in which his communal workers had a guaranteed annual wage. There could not be the compulsion by hunger or need that civilized society utilizes to get unpleasant work done. He felt this work would become attractive if it were infused with gaiety. He believed that two-thirds of little boys and one-third of little girls who are tomboys have a "penchant for filth." They "love to wallow in the mire and play with dirty things." Since they enjoy wreaking havoc and are often unruly, he proposed putting their destructive tendencies to constructive use in service for the community. This group, which he called "Little Hordes," would be autonomous and responsible for loathsome work, whether it were in a slaughterhouse or cleaning a sewer, but they would also be guardians of all animals to see they were not abused. Akin to the Boy Scouts in age and desire for adventure but without adult leadership, the Little Hordes, Fourier argued, would turn the inclinations of young people at present condemned by society—their penchant for dirt and their feelings of pride, insubordination, and impudence—into a service for the state. In return the state would give them honor; all people in authority would give their first salute to the Little Hordes.[21] Fuller did not work out as detailed a plan for the future as Fourier, but she did point out the diversity of male-female inclinations:

In families that I know, some little girls like to saw wood,

others to use carpenters' tools. Where these tastes are in-
dulged, cheerfulness and good-humor are promoted. Where
they are forbidden, because "such things are not proper for
girls," they grow sullen and mischievous.

Fourier had observed these wants of women, as no one can
fail to do who watches the desires of little girls, or knows the
ennui that haunts grown women, except where they make to
themselves a serene little world by art of some kind. He,
therefore, in proposing a great variety of employments, in
manufactures or the care of plants and animals, allows for one
third of women as likely to have a taste for masculine pursuits,
one third of men for feminine. [Pp. 174–175]

She accepted Fourier's view with some modification and reiterated
one of his central psychological concepts: that a person who is
thwarted grows "sullen" and "mischievous," an outward expression
of the internal war of the frustrated self. Charles Fourier's influence,
then, in Margaret Fuller's writing of *Woman* was considerable; she
used aspects of his understanding of the human psychology of both
sexes, attractive industry, liberty of law, and his overall concept of
*l'écart absolu.* Although, as she wrote, she did not accept all of his
methods, she valued and reshaped his hints.

Since Charles Fourier was an acknowledged source for some of
Margaret Fuller's ideas, the question might well be asked to what
extent, if any, she was influenced by other socialists, such as Fanny
Wright, Robert Owen, and his son, Robert Dale Owen. They
attempted radical collective living experiments in the United States
in New Harmony, Indiana, and Nashoba, Tennessee. During
Fuller's youth, these militant social reformers were at the height of
their notoriety because their experiments in communal and interra-
cial living were accompanied with and succeeded by both lectures
and publications promulgating their unorthodox views.

From the summer of 1828 until July 1830 when she sailed for
Europe, Frances Wright organized the New York paper, the *Free
Enquirer,* which succeeded the *New Harmony and Nashoba Gazette.*
When Robert Dale Owen joined her, he took over most of the
editorial work of the paper while she lectured on such subjects as

free public education, organized religion as an affront to reason, female emancipation, birth control, and other radical ideas.[22]

During this time Robert Dale Owen wrote an article, "Of Men and Women," in one of a series of popular tracts that the *Free Enquirer* published in 1830. This short essay contains many of the usual arguments and analogies used in the literature advocating emancipation of women. In the tradition of Mary Wollstonecraft, Owen was forthright in his arguments and interestingly enough introduced his article with an attack on Washington Irving, whom he called "a writer of brilliant, engaging talents, rather than of sound and useful principles." Owen argued that Irving's "The Broken Heart" is a story that "has produced infinite mischief."[23] He stated that this type of story, in which a girl who has been disappointed in love dies of a broken heart, tacitly implied that "woman is formed for the sole—only purpose of gaining man's affections—that she lives but in man's smiles, and dies when these smiles are withdrawn." Owen then attacked society's custom of assigning half of its species to a situation that was neither rational nor natural but instead artificial and injurious. He continued his essay by contending that the same standards of virtue should be applied to women and to men, with the tests of honesty, generosity, independence of spirit, benevolence, and disinterestedness rather than mere chastity. Robert Dale Owen postulated many of the arguments that Mary Wollstonecraft used. But Wollstonecraft attacked the concepts of didactic expository writers, whereas Owen attacked Irving's story as an example of the unfortunate stance of sentimental fiction. Since Fuller was twenty years old at the time this tract was published, it is not inconceivable that she could have seen it. She also considered other moral qualities of women as important as physical chastity, and like Owen, she too discussed a writer's treatment of his heroines in fiction.

Even if she had not read this issue of the *Free Enquirer*, she undoubtedly had heard of Fanny Wright, and it is puzzling that she did not mention her along with Angelina Grimké and Abby Kelly as examples of "women who speak in public." Fuller continued by writing: "if they have a moral power . . . that is, if they speak for conscience' [*sic*] sake, to serve a cause which they hold sacred,—they invariably subdue the prejudices of their hearers, and excite an interest proportionate to the aversion with which it had been the purpose to regard them" (pp. 110–111). Probably the words *moral power* and *sacred* could be construed as part of the reason she chose not to include Fanny Wright as an example of a female public speaker. Although Angelina Grimké, from an aristocratic slaveholding family in South Carolina, was a well-publicized speaker, and Abby Kelly from Lynn, Massachusetts, was lesser known, both women had spoken in public in the antislavery cause. Angelina Grimké and Abby Kelly were more conventionally religious and used Christianity in their abolitionist lectures, whereas Frances Wright was a rationalist opposed to organized religion, who often lectured against tax exemptions for church property and made other attacks on the churches. She was known in the press as "the great Red Harlot of Infidelity" and the "whore of Babylon." In addition to the churches, Wright attacked the whole political system, the tax laws, the banks (which she thought were controlled by European interests), and marriage.[24] Both Angelina Grimké and Abby Kelly were also criticized for their abolitionist sentiments. These opinions were so unpopular in 1838 that when they spoke at an antislavery convention in Philadelphia, their speeches were interrupted by a howling, threatening mob. They used Christian prayers and parables, however, to reinforce their speeches.[25] Wright was also opposed to slavery but was not an abolitionist because she thought that slaves should be emancipated gradually after having been educated and prepared to participate in society.[26] Since she lectured in Boston in August 1829, when Fuller was living in Cambridge and the Reverend Lyman Beecher in one of his sermons on political atheism complained that females of education and refinement were among her votaries, it seems reasonable to believe that Fuller either had heard the lecture or at least had discussed Wright's radical views with her friends.[27] It seems logical to assume, therefore, that Fuller left Wright, the most dramatic of the socialist thinkers, out of *Woman* by design, probably for reasons of conviction or of discretion. She could afford to be more charitable toward Mary Wollstonecraft because she was dead and George Sand because she was French, but Fanny Wright (now Madame D'Arusmont, but separated from her husband) was alive and living in the United States. Her inflammatory lectures were too recent in the public mind.

Instead of calling her an "infidel of the French Revolution" as Lydia Maria Child had done, Fuller may have chosen to make her conspicuous by her absence in *Woman*. Wright might not have appeared to Fuller to have the "moral power" that she believed was necessary for the spiritual regeneration of men and women.

Socialist liberalism was an important influence in the distillation of Fuller's ideas because of the acknowledged influence of Charles Fourier, and the unacknowledged intellectual ferment that Robert Dale Owen and Frances Wright generated. Frances Wright's type of revolutionary fervor came to Margaret Fuller later in Europe as her ideas developed under the tutelege of Adam Mickiewicz and Giuseppe Mazzini. Until then, Mary Wollstonecraft was Fuller's strongest source of argument from rationalist thinkers, which led her to write *Woman in the Nineteenth Century*.

## NOTES

1. George Eliot, "Margaret Fuller and Mary Wollstonecraft," *The Leader* (1855; rpt., *The Norton Anthology of English Literature*, third ed., 1974), 2:1322–1328.

2. *Memoirs of Margaret Fuller Ossoli*, ed. Ralph Waldo Emerson, William Henry Channing, and James Freeman Clarke (Boston: Phillips, Sampson and Company, 1852), 1:14–17.

3. There is a parallel between the lives of Mary Wollstonecraft and Margaret Fuller. Both women were spinsters in their early thirties at the time they wrote their protest pieces. Each woman had to struggle to earn a living in the limited fields open to females at that time, first as teachers and later as writers.

4. Ralph M. Wardle, *Mary Wollstonecraft: A Critical Biography* (Lawrence: University of Kansas Press, 1951), p. 145.

5. Mary Wollstonecraft, *A Vindication of the Rights of Woman*, ed. Charles W. Hagelman, Jr. (1792; rpt., New York: W. W. Norton & Company, 1967), p. 17.

6. Fuller, *Woman in the Nineteenth Century and Kindred Papers Relating to the Sphere, Condition and Duties of Women*, ed. Arthur B. Fuller (Boston: John P. Jewitt, 1855), p. 26.

7. An "old maid" was a social pariah. If any readers have ever played the card game of "old maid," they will recall that the person left with the old maid card was the loser. Today, fortunately, this opprobrious term is going

out of fashion. As Fuller in her use of both terms points out by implication, "old bachelor" was seldom used.

8. Eliot observes Fuller often passes in one breath from "forcible reasoning to dreamy vagueness." Eliot claimed Fuller's mind was like some regions of her American continent, where you step from sunny clearings to the mysterious twilight of the tangled forest. *Norton Anthology*, 2:1323.

9. Wardle, *Wollstonecraft*, pp. 314–318.

10. Margaret Fuller, *Literature and Art* (New York: Fowler and Wells, 1852), pp. 146–147, 142.

11. Donald A. Ringe, *Charles Brockden Brown* (New York: Twayne Publishers, 1964), p. 133.

12. Charles Brockden Brown, *Alcuin: A Dialogue* (1798; rpt., New Haven, 1935), p. 42.

13. Brown started his dialogue between Alcuin, the male schoolteacher, and Mrs. Carter, a widow, who kept a literary and intellectual salon, by having Alcuin ask her: "Pray, Madam, are you a federalist?" Her response initially is the usual feminine dissimulation of pausing, smiling, and finally answering: "You are in jest—shallow and inexperienced as all women are known to be." Once Alcuin convinces Mrs. Carter he is in earnest, she ceases to play a role and discusses the issues, sometimes taking a more radical position than he.

14. Thomas Wentworth Higginson, *Margaret Fuller Ossoli* (Boston: Houghton Mifflin, 1887), p. 180.

15. *Memoirs*, 2:73.

16. Charles Fourier, *Traité de l'association domestique-agricole, Oeuvres Complètes* (1841–1843), rpt. in *The Utopian Vision of Charles Fourier: Selected Texts on Work, Love and Passionate Attraction*, trans. and ed. Jonathan Beecher and Richard Bienvenu (Boston: Beacon Press, 1971), p. 275.

17. Nathaniel Hawthorne to Louisa Hawthorne, May 3, 1841. *Autobiography of Brook Farm*, ed. Henry W. Sams (Englewood Cliffs, N.J.: Prentice-Hall, 1958), p. 18.

18. *Memoirs*, 2:206.

19. Fourier's *Le Nouveau monde amoureux* was not published until 1967 in Paris. This work contains specific discussions of sex orgies, free love, and universal sexual gratification that Fourier advocated.

20. *Le Nouveau monde industriel et sociétaire, Oeuvres Complètes de Charles Fourier*, 3d ed. (Paris, 1848), rpt. in *Utopian Vision of Fourier*, pp. 386–389.

21. *Le Nouveau monde industriel et sociétaire*, rpt. in *Utopian Vision of Fourier*, pp. 317–322.

22. William Randall Waterman, *Frances Wright* (1924; rpt., New York: AMS Press, 1967), pp. 148–178.

23. Robert Dale Owen, "Of Men and Women," Popular tracts, no. 1 (New York: Office of the *Free Inquirer*, 1830), pp. 10–15.

24. Frances Wright, *Views of Society and Manners in America*, ed. Paul R. Baker (Cambridge: Belknap Press of Harvard University Press, 1963), pp. xix–xxi.

25. *History of Woman Suffrage*, ed. Elizabeth Cady Stanton, Susan B. Anthony, and Matilda Joslyn Gage (New York: Fowler & Wells, 1881), 1:334–337.

26. Waterman, *Frances Wright*, pp. 126–129. In her famous experiment in Nashoba, Tennessee, she bought some slaves who were then expected to work in the commune. She advocated their amalgamation with the white race as a solution to the racial problem.

27. Ibid., pp. 178–179.

# Chapter 3 The feminists and their supporters

Margaret Fuller not only adopted ideas from the socialists and rationalists, but she also assimilated ideas from the feminists. Like other crusaders, she robbed any storehouse of ideas that seemed to strengthen her position. Her experience and instinct were the ultimate criteria for her use or rejection of material for *Woman in the Nineteenth Century*. In effect, she was an eclectic pragmatist.

Unlike the English and other American feminists, Fuller was strongly influenced by the European romantic movement. However, she was more than a synthesizer; in many instances she developed an idea or changed its meaning so that it became her own.

The novels that the romantic movement engendered had a disquieting effect upon Margaret Fuller. For the most part, they postulated a role that logically she felt a woman should not have to play. If a woman were indeed a whole person guided by reason, as the Age of Enlightenment had suggested, how could she be ruled by passion, which should be only one aspect of her life rather than her whole life? In *Woman* she wrote: "It is a vulgar error that love, *a* love, to Woman is her whole existence; she also is born for Truth and Love in their universal energy" (p. 177). Hence, her attitude toward Anne Louise Germaine (Necker) Staël-Holstein and Amandine Aurore Lucile (Dupin) Dudevant (George Sand) was one of admiration mingled with some disapproval. These European incarnations of the romantic heroine pursuing her grande passion influenced Fuller as much by their independent life-styles as by their novels.

Fuller has been frequently called the "Yankee Corinne" and even accused of affecting her role.[1] The appeal of love and the rapturous descriptions of Italy in *Corinne* as well as the political intrigue in which Madame de Staël was involved suggested possibilities to Fuller of the exciting life that an independent woman might command. Although she used Madame de Staël as an example of a famous female author, she did not prise her without qualification: "De Staël's name was not so clear of offence; she could not forget the Woman in the thought; while she was instructing you as a mind, she wished to be admired as a Woman; sentimental tears often dimmed the eagle glance" (p. 94). Nevertheless, Fuller recognized the power of the romantic influence that Madame de Staël exerted: "Her intellect, too, with all its splendor, trained in a drawing-room, fed on flattery, was tainted and flawed; yet its beams make the obscurest school-house in New England warmer and lighter to the little rugged girls who are gathered together on its wooden bench" (p. 94). Fuller admired the romantic possibilities for a richer life that Madame de Staël represented while at the same time deploring her sentimentality.

Fuller's attitude toward George Sand was more favorable than toward Madame de Staël. Her defense of the notorious George Sand, although not without some initial qualifications, was a strong stand to take for her time. Both George Sand and Mary Wollstonecraft, she argued, were women whose lives more than anything they wrote proved "the need of some new interpretation of Woman's Rights" (p. 75). Because the social restrictions of their lives were so narrow, these women of genius became outlaws, Fuller explained. Moreover, Fuller excused Sand's unconventional conduct because men left her no alternative: "George Sand smokes, wears male attire, wishes to be addressed as '*Mon frère;*'—perhaps, if she found those who were as brothers indeed, she would not care whether she were brother or sister" (pp. 75–76).

Probably as a conciliatory gesture and as a means of hedging her position, Fuller then interpolated a note about Elizabeth Barrett, "who has precisely the qualities that the author of Simon and Indiana lacks . . . [who is] . . . unblemished in character, so high in aim, and pure in soul." Barrett was not afraid to look for virtue in one "as noble in nature, but clouded by error," she argued, and Fuller included two sonnets recently written by Barrett to George Sand.[2]

Although Fuller conceded that Sand must have experienced great wrong from men, she rejoiced to see that in her romantic novel, *La Roche Mauprat*, Sand had changed her attitude of contempt for men to one of acceptance. *Mauprat* depicts "a man raised by the workings of love from the depths of savage sensualism to a moral and intellectual life" (p. 76). Probably Fuller selected *Mauprat* to discuss because it reinforced her exalted view of the possibilities of married love, as well as her feeling that marriage should not be a commercial transaction. Sand's preface to *Mauprat* makes this idea clear: "The conviction was forced upon me that marriage, to be anything more than a mere name, must embody principles of happiness and justice which are too elevated in their nature for actual society to be interested about them."[3] In addition to Sand's expression of her high ideals for marriage, Fuller also must have admired Sand's thesis in *Mauprat*—that a man should be as chaste as a woman—because it is in accord with her oft-expressed view in *Woman*.

Next Fuller prophesied a better era for women such as Sand, while at the same time she referred to Sand's flaws:

> But women like Sand will speak now and cannot be silenced; their characters and their eloquence alike foretell an era when such as they shall easier learn to lead true lives. But though such forebode, not such shall be parents of it. Those who would reform the world must show that they do not speak in the heat of wild impulse; their lives must be unstained by passionate error: they must be severe lawgivers to themselves. [P. 77]

Again in a later discussion, she criticized Sand: "Even George Sand, who would trample on every graceful decorum, and every human law, for the sake of a sincere life, does not see that she violates it by making her heroines able to tell falsehoods in a good cause" (p. 149).

Alternating criticism and defense, Fuller approved of Sand as much as she dared. An interpretation of Fuller's motive as a political tactic is indicated because her subsequent comments gradually become less critical and more complimentary, until her position culminates in unqualified approbation.

A lessening in her judgmental moral stance is apparent in her discussion of Sand's *Lettres d'un Voyageur*, in which she deplored Sand's weakness in bewailing her loneliness and her need to write for money. Concluding that Sand was "no self-ruling Aspasia," she nevertheless believed Sand possessed genius and a writing style that burned with "a deeply smouldering fire" (pp. 229–230). In another essay, "French Novelists of the Day," printed in the *New York Tribune*, February 1, 1845, Fuller calmly began her discussion by mentioning Sand's masculine clothing and her illicit connections with men. She excused her conduct by explaining that Sand did not wish to be a hypocrite, but Sand, like Mary Stuart, could say: "Though I have erred, I am better than my reputation." Then Fuller employed a surgical metaphor that Sand had dared to probe her country's festering wounds—"Would, indeed, the surgeon had come with quite clean hands." Nevertheless, she admired her work, which she felt displayed great descriptive and poetic talent, as vigorous in conception. With her usual acute critical acumen, however, Fuller considered Sand's best works uneven, obviously written in haste, with careless or flagging spirits (pp. 231–236).

Seven months later, in another piece, "Jenny Lind, the Consuelo of George Sand," printed again in the daily *New York Tribune*, Fuller made fewer excuses for Sand's conduct and praised her *Consuelo* as a book of "rare value." She drew at some length parallels between the life of Sand's protagonist in *Consuelo* and the Swedish singer, Jenny Lind. Sand, she observed, was a "glowing genius," whose treatment of religion and philosophy was clumsy compared with her command of poetry and rhetoric. Interesting this time is her change of attitude toward Sand's notoriety; she considered her a truth seeker, an exponent "of the difficulties, the errors, the aspirations, the weaknesses, and the regenerative powers" of her epoch. In remarks that must have enraged many of her readers, Fuller boldly declared that Sand, with her sensual nature, was peculiarly fitted to speak to men, "so diseased as men are at present" (pp. 241–249).

Her June 24, 1846, review of *Consuelo* is a striking example of either the evolution of Fuller's thinking as a critic or her view that her radical position was now tenable. At any rate, she did not apologize for Sand's behavior but declared that the true facts of her life were not known, that she had heard too much gossip to believe it as reliable about any one. She knew Sand through her works as a soul capable of goodness and honor. But what is important is that Fuller asserted, "It is her works, and not her private life, that we are considering. Of her works we have means of judging; of herself, not" (p. 239). Fuller assumed a critical position that is now taken for granted by literary critics but that in her time was unusual—that the private life of an artist is no one else's business.

Six months after her review appeared, Fuller went to great lengths to secure an interview with Sand in Paris. At this time she wrote to Elizabeth Hoar:

> As our eyes met, she said, *"C'est vous,"* and held out her hand. I took it, and went into her little study; we sat down a moment, then I said, *"Il me fait de bien de vous voir,"* and I am sure I said it with my whole heart, for it made me very happy to see such a woman, so large and so developed a character, and everything that is good in it so *really* good. I loved, shall always love her.[4]

In a private letter describing her meeting with George Sand, Fuller disregarded the defense she used in *Woman* to qualify her position relative to Sand and, in fact, asserted: "She needs no defense."[5]

George Sand's English counterparts, Anna Jameson and Harriet Martineau, however, were more interested in social reform than in sex and in the discreet conduct of their lives were closely akin to the American feminists, Catharine Maria Sedgwick and Lydia Maria Francis Child. Of the feminists who influenced Fuller, probably Anna Jameson was the most typical in her carefully crafted psychological presentation of unpopular ideas. Fuller's characteristic way of handling the variety of material she found in Jameson's books was to borrow what she needed and then to extend the meaning to suit her thesis in *Woman*. Jameson (less outspoken than her eighteenth-century country-woman, Mary Wollstonecraft) chose an epigraph from the *Faerie Queene* for her book, *Winter Studies and Summer Rambles in Canada*. This epigraph epitomizes her lifetime method of writing for the advancement of women:

> And over that same door was likewise writ,
> *Be bold, Be bold,* and everywhere *Be bold;*

That much she mus'd, yet could not construe it
By any riddling skill or common wit:
At last she spied at that room's upper end
Another iron door, on which was writ,
*Be not too bold.*[6]

Nevertheless, Fuller was "bold" in that she brought to their logical culmination ideas with which Jameson flirted. Moreover, Jameson's writing contained inconsistencies of thinking, characterized by realism and excessive sentimentality, often juxtaposed. She used sentiment as a mask to hide her aggression and to make her views more acceptable. But at times Jameson herself did not seem to realize the incongruity of her views. Fuller, however, did recognize this division in her thinking:

Mrs. Jameson is a sentimentalist, and, therefore, suits us ill in some respects, but she is full of talent, has a just and refined perception of the beautiful, and a genuine courage when she finds it necessary. She does not appear to have thought out, thoroughly, the subject on which we are engaged, and her opinions, expressed as opinions, are sometimes inconsistent with one another. [P. 131][7]

Jameson's first publication, *Diary of an Ennuyée* (1826), illustrates the sentimentality and inconsistency of which Fuller complained. She adopted the persona of a lovesick young girl during an exhausting tour of Europe: "Could I but become as insensible, as regardless of the painful past as I am of the all lovely present! Why was I proud of my victory over passion? alas! what avails it that I have shaken the viper from my hand, if I have no miraculous antidote against the venom which has mingled with my life-blood, and clogged the pulses of my heart!"[8] Such florid exclamations of the sentimental heroine dying for love are blended into a kind of pastiche with shrewd observations about the people she observes and with excessive travelogue-type descriptions of nature.

After the success of her *Diary*, Jameson continued writing books concerned with women: *Memoirs of the Loves of the Poets* (1829), *Memoirs of Celebrated Female Sovereigns* (1831), and *The Characteristics of Women* (1832).[9] These early works show an evolution in her thinking about feminist topics as she gradually became bolder. Her publication of *Winter Studies and Summer Rambles in Canada* (1838) contained her most outspoken social comments.

Fuller singled out for praise two of Jameson's works in *Woman:* "but from the refined perception of character, admirable suggestions are given in her 'Women of Shakespeare,' and 'Loves of the Poets' " (p. 131). Jameson's early tentative method can be seen in *Memoirs of the Loves of the Poets.* In her preface she was modest: "These little sketches (they can pretend to no higher title) are submitted to the public with a feeling of timidity almost painful . . . to illustrate a subject . . . the influence which the beauty and virtue of women have exercised over the characters and writings of men of genius. Will it be thought unfeminine or obtrusive, if I add yet a few words?"[10]

Despite the fact that Fuller did not mention *Memoirs of Celebrated Female Sovereigns*, it is likely that she had read it because she cited Semiramis, queen of Assyria, Queen Elizabeth, and Catharine of Russia (p. 47), all treated by Jameson. Furthermore, Fuller's appraisal of Queen Elizabeth was not magnanimous—though she conceded respect for her strength—and that of Mary Stuart was more charitable, opinions not too dissimilar from Jameson's. In her preface to this book, Jameson was self-effacing with a thesis that women make poor rulers:

> On the whole, it seems indisputable that the experiments hitherto made in the way of female government have been signally unfortunate; and that women called to empire have been, in most cases conspicuously unhappy or criminal. So that, were we to judge by the past, it might be decided at once, that the power which belongs to us as a sex, is not properly, or naturally, that of the sceptre or the sword.[11]

On the other hand, Fuller's epigraph, "The earth waits for her Queen," expresses the opposite belief—not only could a woman rule, but a queen should rule. In her discussion of Queen Victoria, Fuller also contended that if a queen is trained by adverse circumstances to know the world and her own powers, she could be a queen indeed (p. 108).

Although Fuller knew Shakespeare from her earliest childhood, she recommended Jameson's study of Shakespeare's women for its insight into character. Again in her preface, however, Jameson made sly hints about the status of women and then quickly hedged her position in a twenty-nine-page prefatory debate between a fictional woman, Alda, and a man, Medon. Although these characters talk about a more important role for women, in essence this dialogue, which takes place in a library, is what Clara Thomas calls a "masterpiece of fence-sitting,"[12] as illustrated by the following exchange: "Medon. I presume you have written a book to maintain the superiority of your sex over ours. . . . Alda. But as to maintaining the superiority, or speculating on the rights of women—nonsense! Why should you suspect me of such folly?—it is quite out of date. Why should there be competition or comparison?"[13] This ironic game of postulation and disavowal continues to an inconclusion. There is a trace of this type of dissimulation at the beginning of *Woman*: "Without enrolling ourselves at once on either side, let us look upon the subject from the best point of view which to-day offers; no better, it is to be feared, than a high house-top" (p. 31).

In addition to having adapted to a limited extent Jameson's method of allaying her readers' fears of the consequences of her radical position, Fuller also acknowledged Jameson as the source for the Indian legend she recounted of the woman betrothed to the sun (p. 101). Jameson's chief contribution, Fuller wrote, was her sympathetic treatment of the problems of prostitutes, for which Fuller said she most respected her because "she speaks on a subject which refined women are usually afraid to approach, for fear of the insult and scurrile jest they may encounter" (p. 131). Comparison of both texts indicates that Fuller was indeed indebted to Jameson on this subject. Her method of handling Jameson's material was to extend its meaning, often in a form of exhortation. Jameson wrote:

> We are told openly by moralists and politicians, that it is for the general good of society, nay, an absolute necessity, that one-fifth part of our sex should be condemned as the legitimate prey of the other, predoomed to die in reprobation, in the streets, in hospitals, that the virtue of the rest may be preserved, and the pride and the passions of men both gratified.[14]

Fuller's anger with arguments condoning prostitution was similar to Jameson's: "I refer to the degradation of a large portion of women into the sold and polluted slaves of men, and the daring with which the legislator and man of the world lifts his head beneath the heavens, and says, 'This must be; it cannot be helped; it is a necessary accompaniment of *civilization*' " (p. 132). Jameson first made the startling suggestion that women must face the issue in order that a remedy may be found: "The subject is a hateful one—more hateful is it to hear it sometimes alluded to with sneering levity, and sometimes waved aside with a fastidious or arrogant prudery. Unless we women take some courage to look upon the evil, and find some help, some remedy within ourselves, I know not where it is to come from."[15] Fuller developed Jameson's idea into a direct plea to women to help prostitutes:

> I would urge upon those women who have not yet considered this subject, to do so. Do not forget the unfortunates who dare not cross your guarded way. If it do not suit you to act with those who have organized measures of reform, then hold not yourself excused from acting in private. Seek out these degraded women, give them tender sympathy, counsel, employment. Take the place of mothers, such as might have saved them originally. [P. 147]

Both writers agreed that the men's sin brought on its own punishment. Jameson was ironic: "But I have a bitter pleasure in thinking that this most base, most cruel conventional law is avenged upon those who made and uphold it; that here the sacrifice of a certain number of one sex to the permitted license of the other is no general good, but a general curse—a very ulcer in the bosom of society."[16] Fuller's message was in the style of a sermon: "O wretched men, your sin is its own punishment! You have lost the world in losing yourselves. Who ruins another has admitted the worm to the root of his own tree, and the fuller ye fill the cup of evil, the deeper must be your own bitter draught" (p. 132). Fuller then broadened Jameson's thoughts in that she demanded as equally high standards of chastity from men as from women: "They begin to ask whether virtue is not possible, perhaps necessary, to Man as well as to Woman" (p. 148). Her method of using ideas she had gleaned from her sources was to accept the idea and then to extend its meaning—in this case, to recognize that the problem of prostitution was not going to be solved until men, not just women, changed. Horace Greeley commended her for her courage in speaking of prostitution in mixed circles and wrote that while "others were willing to pity and deplore; Margaret was more inclined to vindicate and redeem."[17] Fuller's attitude was much as Greeley described it. The distinction here seems to be that all of the feminists who were willing to discuss prostitution at all—Wollstonecraft, Jameson, Martineau—agreed that society should take a more sympathetic attitude toward prostitutes and that women who married for money were no better than prostitutes, but Fuller contended that ladies with greater advantages were worse than prostitutes if they did not use their talents properly and help their fallen sisters.[18] She added to her discussion the idea that "the passions, like fire, are a bad master" (p. 154) and that men no less than women should control them.

Less than two years after having written *Woman*, Fuller reacted to Jameson's sentimental inconsistency with outright irritation. In a *New York Tribune* review of a collection of six long essays by Jameson, *Memoirs and Essays, Illustrative of Art, Literature, and Social Morals*, Fuller's language reflected her experience as a practicing journalist as she begins her article with a note of sarcasm. "Mrs. Jameson appears to be growing more and more desperately modest, if we may judge from the motto" (p. 288), she wrote, as she quoted the first stanza of the epigraph:

> What if the little rain should say,
>    "So small a drop as I
> Can ne'er refresh the thirsty plain,—
>    I'll tarry in the sky?"

Castigating Jameson's disclaimers, Fuller commented that the time had passed for this type of affectation or the pretense that a book had been written at the urging of friends. Indeed Jameson was no humble flower. Fuller continued by complaining of the shallowness and inaccuracy in her first essay about Titian, as well as in the one concerning Adelaide Kemble.

What Fuller did find to praise in Jameson's collection was "Woman's Mission and Woman's Position." Fuller rejoiced in this essay in which the author spoke the truth in a straightforward

manner, and she recommended reading it to the "unthinking, wil-
fully [sic] unseeing million" who act as if life for the majority of
women really was "one of protection, and the gentle offices of
home." The "rhetorical" gentlemen and "silken" dames forgot that
the washerwomen, seamstresses, and prostitutes, whom they saw
daily in the streets, were not treated "like cherished flowers in the
garden of domestic love" (p. 292). She then advised her readers not
to look at the ideal of a woman's sphere as one which is protected but
at the reality—at the condition of women in the agricultural and
manufacturing districts in England. Then, after quoting a long
passage from Jameson on this topic, Fuller concluded, "Amen."

She ended her evaluation of Jameson's book, as she had begun,
with a note of sarcasm. Fuller thought that if conditions for governesses were as unfortunate as Jameson averred in "On the Relative
Social Position of Mothers and Governesses," then her advice to
them was unintentionally ironic. Governesses might as well be
"burnt at the stake at once, rather than submit to this slow process of
petrifaction" (p. 294). In her verdict of July 24, 1846, Fuller was
caustic; she concluded that she must go to England to investigate
conditions for herself.

The other British feminist who influenced Margaret Fuller's ideas
in her shaping of *Woman* was Harriet Martineau, with whom she
became acquainted when this well-known English writer toured the
United States in 1835. In fact, Fuller had originally planned to
return to England with Martineau's party but was unable to make
the trip due to the death of her father.[19] She was influenced,
therefore, by her acquaintance with Martineau, during which time
both writers undoubtedly would have discussed the problems facing
women, and by Martineau's books in which she forthrightly discussed the emancipation of women.

In a pattern that is typical in Fuller's composition of *Woman*, she
commented not on Martineau's books but directly on Martineau as a
woman who is influential and cheering to many people. She cited
Martineau and Barrett as examples of women who needed "not
health or youth, or the charms of personal presence, to make their
thoughts available," but were able to exert influence from their sick
rooms (pp. 164-165). There is evidence in *Woman*, however, that she
also borrowed some of her ideas. Martineau's short chapter, "Politi-

cal Non-Existence of Women," from *Society in America* contains the
most rational exposition of the need for women's rights written by
these feminists. Its major premise is: "One of the fundamental
principles announced in the Declaration of Independence is, that
governments derive their just powers from the consent of the
governed."[20] From this premise, she concluded with devastating
logic that because women have not given their consent, their treatment in the United States is not consonant with the principles of
democracy. Next Martineau discussed the rationalizations that men
used to deprive women of their political rights. Even such principled
democratic writers as Thomas Jefferson in America and James Mill
in England had no plausible answer for her and became advocates of
despotism. She then refuted their arguments bluntly, ending with a
comparison of the situation of women with the ridicule that concepts
of democracy once engendered. The idea of a commoner ruling
evoked laughter in Europe; yet no one dared to laugh at Washington
when he became president. Thus is it with the plight of women,
Martineau concluded, as she reiterated her premise from the Declaration of Independence.[21] Fuller also brought in a quotation derived
from the Declaration of Independence—"All men are born free and
equal" (p. 26)—although she did not develop this point to the extent
Martineau did because her writing style was much less direct.

Fuller also accepted as valid some points that Martineau raised
regarding relative standards of treatment of females in the United
States and Europe. When she discussed the lives of women whom
she had observed on her protracted visit, Martineau thought that the
American treatment of women not only did not live up to democratic principles but also fell below the practice of some parts of the Old
World. She further contended:

> The unconsciousness of both parties as to the injuries suffered
> by women at the hands of those who hold the power is a
> sufficient proof of the low degree of civilisation in this impor-
> tant particular at which they rest. While woman's intellect is
> confined, her morals crushed, her health ruined, her weakness-
> es encouraged, and her strength punished, she is told that her
> lot is cast in the paradise of women: and there is no country in
> the world where there is so much boasting of the "chivalrous"
> treatment she enjoys.[22]

Fuller wrote, however, that women in the United States "are in
many respects, better situated than men" (p. 109). Because ladies
were not weighed down by demands for success, they had more time
for books and meditation. Then, however, Fuller adopted a position
similar to Martineau's. With inductive logic, Martineau argued:

> She has the best place in stage-coaches: when there are not
> chairs enough for everybody, the gentlemen stand: she hears
> oratorical flourishes on public occasions about wives and
> home, and apostrophes to woman: her husband's hair stands
> on end at the idea of her working, and he toils to indulge her
> with money . . . her morals are guarded by the strictest obser-
> vance of propriety in her presence. In short, indulgence is
> given her as a substitute for justice.[23]

This is characteristic of Martineau's writing—many details leading
to a rapier-like conclusion. Fuller used the same ideas but developed
them deductively:

> She has already learned that all bribes have the same flaw; that
> truth and good are to be sought for their own sakes. . . . Men
> are very courteous to them. They praise them often, check
> them seldom. There is chivalry in the feeling toward "the
> ladies," which gives them the best seats in the stage-coach,
> frequent admission, not only to lectures of all sorts, but to
> courts of justice, halls of legislature, reform conventions.
> [P. 110]

In comparing her writing with that of Martineau, it seems evident
that Fuller was indebted to her, in this case even to her use of the
example of stagecoach gallantry.

When *Society in America* was first published, Fuller wrote to
Martineau complaining of her "intemperate tirade" against Bronson
Alcott and of her excessive abolitionism on "almost every page."[24]
Fuller's writing is much more complex; at times it is ironical and
subtle, whereas Martineau's observations are more uniform and
straightforward. The reason may be that Fuller's goals were broader
than Martineau's. Ultimately Fuller was concerned with spiritual
fulfillment, while Martineau was interested in social progress.

Hence, in order to express the need to find unity with the cosmos, Fuller, like other writers before her, had to turn to symbol.

There were three American advocates of the feminist cause—John Neal, Catharine Maria Sedgwick, and Lydia Maria Child—who also left their mark on the formation of *Woman in the Nineteenth Century*. John Neal, from Portland, Maine, was a journalist and early lecturer who worked for female emancipation.[25] Neal's influence on Fuller derived from his lecture on the destiny and vocation of woman, which he gave in Providence at the Greene Street School when she was a teacher there. He made a strong impression on her, as she confided to her journal, and gave early encouragement to her interest in women's rights. She did not forget Neal; she sent him a copy of *Woman* some years later when it was published.[26] Of major importance, however, is the most innocuous feminist, Catharine Maria Sedgwick, who led a blameless personal life and, unlike Lydia Maria Child, was not a militant abolitionist. Fuller praised Sedgwick's character as a model to emulate and valued her books for the practical advice they gave in the art of self-help and virtuous living. But she did cite Child as an example of a woman who took a brave stand.

The literary output of both Sedgwick and Child shows the influence of their Puritan heritage, with its didactic strain and its emphasis on duty, thrift, and hard work. Both women wrote popular novels (Sedgwick's *Redwood* and Child's *Hobomok*) as well as advice books that were designed to help housewives cope with domestic problems. For example, Child's *The Frugal Housewife* is a combination cookbook and home nursing handbook, and her *The Mother's Book* gives advice on how to raise children, emphasizing the problems related to educating girls. A study of the writing of both authors indicates that they gradually became concerned with larger issues confronting women, such as the unmarried woman's need to earn a better living, the housewife's problems with a drunkard husband, or the personal tragedy of girls who yielded to social pressure to get married and made unsuitable matches.[27]

Of the feminists who inspired her, Catharine Maria Sedgwick, by Fuller's own admission in *Woman*, was the "clearest, wisest, and kindliest, who has, as yet, used pen here on these subjects" (p. 163).

During the first half of the nineteenth century, Sedgwick "would doubtless have been considered the queen of American letters."[28] Her first publication in 1822 was intended as little more than a religious tract, but it outgrew the dimensions of a tract and developed into "A New England Tale." However, it was *Live and Let Live: or Domestic Service Illustrated* that was highly praised by William Ellery Channing. Openly didactic, this volume contains sensible advice for ladies, mostly in regard to their relationship with servants. With a literary allusion to *Hamlet,* she entitled chapter 7 "To Cure, or to Endure—That Is the Question." This chapter contains an appeal to enlightened self-interest by contending that if the mistress is kind to her servants, they will respond and be more effective workers: "I most certainly benefit myself by promoting the improvement of those under my care."[29] Women should not be ignorant and therefore be at the mercy of their servants; they should learn how to do household tasks in order to train their servants and, if without domestic help, to be self-reliant and able to function by themselves. Instead of denigrating housework, Sedgwick believed that it was worthy of a lady: "Other things being equal, the woman of the highest mental endowments will always be the best house-keeper, for housewifery, domestic economy, is a science that brings into action the qualities of the mind or will as the graces of the heart."[30] Her purpose in writing the book, she announced in her preface, was to give menial household tasks a more exalted role—to "incite even a few of my young countrywomen to a zealous devotion to 'home missions.' "

Sedgwick illustrated her thesis with examples of famous women. Fuller followed a similar practice in *Woman.* As models of famous ladies who were good housewives, Sedgwick cited Andromache and Desdemona as "heroines to redeem domestic offices from their vulgarity, to *idealize* the housewife."[31] Why she selected these two ill-fated women as examples for girls to emulate is difficult to understand, except that they were properly submissive wives of high rank, devoted to their husbands. Sedgwick also chose Madame Roland as a model wife. Her point was that housework must not only be done with grace but also with efficiency, again reiterating the value of the Puritan work ethic: "She [Madame Roland] administered family affairs with a very small income, and she was at the head of an immense establishment, and in both positions she says her domestic duties were comprised within two hours."[32]

Fuller also chose the ill-fated Madame Roland as a model. Moreover, she used Sedgwick herself as "a fine example of the independent and beneficent existence that intellect and character can given to Woman, no less than Man, if she know how to seek and prize it,—also, that the intellect need not absorb or weaken, but rather will refine and invigorate, the affections,—the teachings of her practical good sense come with great force, and cannot fail to avail much" (p. 163).

*Live and Let Live* also hints at the social concerns that later were to interest Fuller: "Surely the time will come in this country, where the elements of general prosperity have not been destroyed by the foolish combinations and wicked monopolies of men, when the poor will have less need of passive virtues."[33] It is replete with Franklinesque homilies and hints for getting on in the world for both mistress and maid—for example, "Perfection bears with imperfection." "Do not let us consider any occupation so vulgar as indolence and inanity." As a frame for her advice, Sedgwick interpolated a slender love story, a type of "Poor Lucy Lee's Almanac," of how to advance from domestic to housewife.[34] Poor Lucy is a modest Cinderella, a female Horatio Alger who marries the baker's son and moves up to a prosperous but hard-working future in Ohio.

Sedgwick's other book with a compound title, *Means and Ends, or Self-Training*, is a more important influence in the composition of *Woman*. With an allusion to Sedgwick's title, Fuller praised this book for its wholesome suggestions for better health: "Every way her writings please me both as to means and ends. I am pleased at the stress she lays on observance of the physical laws, because the true reason is given. Only in a strong and clean body can the soul do its message fitly" (p. 163). Dedicated to her young countrywomen, *Means and Ends* contains a chapter devoted to women's rights, clearly entitled "The Rights of Women." This last chapter, which seems to contain the conclusion to which all of the others were leading, centered on the questions: How should I live as a woman? What can I do? Unlike *Live and Let Live*, *Means and Ends* has no Cinderella tale to give it framework or love interest. Instead chapters are organized around such topics as education, forethought, health, care of skin, exercise, housewifery, dress, gossiping, calumny and evil reports, what to read, and love of nature—typical subjects for later magazines that were designed for women. Sedgwick, like other feminists, recognized the need to make women's clothing more comfortable. Fuller mistakenly mentioned as a sign of the times that women were giving up corsets and then concluded: "Yes! let us give up all artificial means of distortion. Miss Sedgwick, in teaching that domestics must have the means of bathing as much as their mistresses, and time, too, to bathe, has symbolized one of the most important of human rights" (p. 164).

At first glance, however, Sedgwick's thesis in her chapter dealing with women's rights seems somewhat puzzling because it usually connotes a military reality: "*Your might must make your right.*" She explained her meaning in this way: "By this, I mean that you must qualify yourselves for the exercise of higher powers than women have yet possessed, before they can be entrusted to you; and that, when you are thus qualified, they cannot long be withheld from you."[35] Fuller recognized that Sedgwick thought there should be no limits to what women could do despite the fact that Sedgwick disavowed any interest in the ballot, legislature, or judgeships for women: "Miss Sedgwick, though she inclines to the private path, and wishes that, by the cultivation of character, might should vindicate right, sets limits nowhere, and her objects and inducements are pure" (p. 163).

Apparently Sedgwick followed the pattern of other early feminists. It was at first to disavow any intentions of upsetting the established social order: "My dear young friends, nothing is farther from my intentions than to make you the bold asserters of your own rights, and the noisy proclaimers of your own powers." She followed her disavowal by suggesting that women educate themselves to act rationally because at present they used only half of their powers. Again she hastily retreated from the implications of her position: "I pray you not to misunderstand me. I am far enough from wishing to encroach on man's sphere. It has been well and truly said, that 'when a woman claims the rights of a man, she surrenders her own rights.' "[36] In *Woman* Fuller used similar methods to reassure her readers: "But were this freedom to come suddenly, I have no fear of the consequences. Individuals might commit excesses, but there is not only in the sex a reverence for decorums and limits inherited and enhanced from generation to generation, which many years of other life could not efface, but a native love, in Woman as Woman, of proportion" (p. 173). Sedgwick, however, again contradicted herself by giving as an illustration of her desire not to claim a man's rights the story of a girl who was able to keep a set of books competently without losing her "feminine delicacy." Mary Bond, her example, so impressed her brother with the accuracy of her accounts that she won his confidence. Henceforth, her brother, Raymond, held faith in a woman's abilities, unshaken by argument or ridicule. Moving from this point with her example of the competent bookkeeper, she quickly brought in her belief that Raymond would then understand that a widow could manage her own property and that a wife has the right to separate from a drunkard and retain custody of her children. With the inspiration of such a sister before him, Sedgwick asserted the brother would be able to withstand the "allurement of vicious women," that he would disdain the society of empty-headed, frivolous, and "gossiping girls" and not "run the slightest risk of yoking himself to an uneducated girl, however beautiful, high-born, rich and fashionable." She concluded her sanguine view of a sister's influence by reasserting her military thesis, now in the future tense: *"Your might will enforce your right."* Fuller, however, did not acknowledge Sedgwick's inconsistency: "Her speech is moderate and sane, but never palsied by fear or skeptical caution" (p. 163).

Margaret Fuller was more realistic than to expect a sister to influence her brother to the extent that he would rationally choose a good wife. She did, however, accept both the *means* Catharine Maria Sedgwick suggested—self-improvement and competence which would force men to grant women their rights—and her ends—growth—as Sedgwick defined her terms in her conclusion: "You must take your own training into your own hands . . . the mainspring is within. If that works, there is life, growth, and upward progress. Again and again, I repeat it, there are none educated but the self-educated."[37] Sedgwick, and later Fuller in *Woman*, stressed the importance of the inner self, self-reliance, and the possibility of growth as a means for women to realize their goals.

Although Margaret Fuller did not praise Lydia Maria Child as highly as she did Catharine Maria Sedgwick—and mentioned her directly only once in *Woman*—there is both textual evidence and the evidence of their long friendship to suggest that Child's influence on Fuller's thinking, and hence on the composition of *Woman*, was considerable. Instead of discussing her writing, however, Fuller praised Child's support of Amelia Norman, who was accused of trying to stab her seducer on the steps of the Astor House. Amelia Norman's case was notorious at the time, and Child not only went to her trial but also took her into her own home after she was acquitted. Furthermore, she supported her cause publicly by writing editorials on the need for laws against seducers.[38] Fuller expressed her admiration for Child's actions in *Woman*:

> I must in this place mention, with respect and gratitude, the conduct of Mrs. Child in the case of Amelia Norman. The action and speech of this lady was of straightforward nobleness, undeterred by custom or cavil from duty toward an injured sister. She showed the case and the arguments the counsel against the prisoner had the assurance to use in their true light to the public. She put the case on the only ground of religion and equity. She was successful in arresting the attention of many who had before shrugged their shoulders, and let sin pass as necessarily a part of the company of men. They begin to ask whether virtue is not possible, perhaps necessary, to Man as well as to Woman. [P. 148]

As she had praised Sedgwick for her character, so she commended Child for her bravery in her unusual defense.

As a result of their long friendship, Fuller also absorbed some of Child's other ideas. At one of the most impressionable ages, seventeen, Fuller first became acquainted with Lydia Maria Francis in Watertown, Massachusetts. Eight years older, though not yet married, Lydia Maria Francis was already a well-known novelist. In her diary for January 10, 1827, Fuller characterized Francis as a "most interesting woman," natural, and free from cant and pretension. The adolescent Margaret found in her the ideal woman she was seeking. Together they pored over the lives and works of John Locke, Madame de Staël, and Madame Roland.[39] Later Child was to develop some of this material into one of her series of biographies written for the Ladies Library, *Biographies of Mme. de Staël and Mme. Roland* (1832)[40]. In this series she also had published in the same year *Biographies of Lady Russell and Mme. Guion*. It is of interest in a study of Fuller's sources that except for Madame Guion, Fuller used all of them in *Woman* as models of exceptional women.

Lydia Francis, then, served as an encouragement to the young Margaret Fuller when they first studied together the careers of illustrious women noted for their brilliance, courage, and independence of action rather than for their beauty. It is not surprising, therefore, that Fuller also developed some of the data appearing in Child's *History of the Condition of Women* when she wrote her own feminist treatise.[41] Child's work contains some historical accounts, but it is more like anthropology than history, with its descriptions of the way women have lived in many societies. Child's sources were numerous, ranging from Plutarch, the Bible, and Xenophon to more contemporary works such as Heckewelder's travel journals. She recounted the tales of two devoted married couples described by Xenophon. The story of Panthea, Cyrus's captive, and her husband, Abradatus, is given in both Child's *History* and in Fuller's *Woman* (pp. 85-91). So too is the tale of the Armenian prince, Tigranes, and his wife recounted both in the *History* and in *Woman* (pp. 91–92). Fuller quoted some of the story directly from Xenophon's *Cyropadia*, but the point is that she probably chose these tales either because she was reminded of them from the *History* or because she had discussed them with Child. In addition, Fuller used the story of the Countess Emily Plater as an example of a Polish Joan of Arc (p. 45), a tale that is also in Child's *History*.[42]

Child's *History*, written as a human-interest kind of journalism, sold well. Focusing on the circumstances of a woman's lot, her history covered a dazzling succession of cultures, starting with the Hebrew.[43] Lydia Maria Child generally answered questions about a society's attitude toward women: Was there any courtship before marriage? Did a girl have any voice in the choice of her husband? Did she have a dowry or did her husband buy her? What type of marriage ceremony and festivities took place? How was the bride dressed? Did the wife have any control over her children? Was female infanticide practiced? Was divorce possible? If so, under what circumstances? What punishment for adultery was there for the guilty wife, and was there any punishment for an adulterous husband? In the case of polygamy, what rights, if any, did the old wife have? When a woman was widowed, what became of her? Was she expected to die in suttee with her husband's corpse, or could she remarry? Could she inherit property or was she wholly under the control of her eldest son? In addition to answering these questions, Child recounted numerous anecdotes and legends from her variety of sources.

Child tended to dwell on two aspects of problems related to women, the more dramatic of which was life in the harem. Descriptions of life in the seraglio whether in Persia or Arabia were given in as much detail as she could cull. Her other interest (reminiscent of Harriet Martineau) was chattel slavery, no doubt because of her devout support of the abolitionist movement. This concern was never far from the surface in describing women both in Africa and in the United States: "One of the worst features of this polluting system is that female slaves are neither protected by law, or restrained by public opinion." When she described the institution of slavery, Child tended to editorialize and give a more explicit point of view of its evil than she did in discussing the treatment of women in general. At times her vivid descriptions of people and places sound detached, but at other times, she did make a point: "Jests at the expense of women prevail in Turkey, as they do all over the world."[44] This type of remark inserted occasionally was presented more as a fact than as a polemic.

When Child did venture some interpretation of her findings on the condition of women throughout the world toward the end of volume 2, she was circumspect:[45]

> At those periods, when reason has run wild, and men have maintained that there was no such thing as unchangeable truth, but that everyone make it, according to the state of his own will—at such times, there has always been a tendency to have men and women change places, that the latter might command armies and harangue senates, while men attended to domestic concerns. These doctrines were maintained by infidels of the French revolution, and by their modern disciple, Fanny Wright.

Many silly things have been written and are now written,
concerning the equality of the sexes; but that true and perfect
companionship, which gives both man and woman complete
freedom *in* their places, without a restless desire to go out of
them, is as yet imperfectly understood. The time will come,
when it will be seen that the moral and intellectual condition of
woman must be, and ought to be, in exact correspondence
with that of man, not only in its general aspect, but in its
individual manifestations; and then it will be perceived that all
this discussion about relative superiority, is as idle as a controversy to determine which is most important to the world,
the light of the sun, or the warmth of the sun.[46]

Again as with the other feminists (except for Martineau), Child was
cautious in presenting her ideas. Moreover, in the preface to *An
Appeal in Favor of That Class of Americans Called Africans*, she admitted
she should have been attending to her household concerns, but she
nevertheless did make the appeal.[47] As with many other women,
Child was more willing to be brave in her appeal for the slaves'
emancipation than for her own.

What is significant as far as *The History of the Condition of Women in
Various Ages and Nations* is concerned is not Child's occasional general
comment but her selection of facts. She presented her point of view
by what she included in her *History*—details of the methods the
Chinese used to bind their little girls' feet or how the Hindu society
induced a widow to burn herself on the funeral pyre with her
husband's corpse. Fuller took this mass of material and interpreted
it. Both women suggested that there was not as much difference
between life in a harem and their own lives as Western women
would have liked to believe. Child wrote: "This influence has extended a considerable degree to America; and mothers are not
wanting who will consent to sell their daughters to the highest
bidder, though the bargain is accompanied with formalities, supposed to render it more respectable than the sale of Circassian girls
in the Turkish markets."[48] Fuller editorialized:

Centuries have passed since, but civilized Europe is still in a
transition state about marriage; not only in practice but in

thought. It is idle to speak with contempt of the nations where polygamy is an institution, or seraglios a custom, while practices far more debasing haunt, well-nigh fill, every city and every town, and so far as union of one with one is believed to be the only pure form of marriage, a great majority of societies and individuals are still doubtful whether the earthly bond must be a meeting of souls, or only supposes a contract of convenience and utility. Were Woman established in the rights of an immortal being, this could not be. [Pp. 70–71]

Fuller condemned the practices of civilized Europe as worse than those in polygamous societies and argued that until women had their rights, they would not be free in their choices of husbands.

Like the other feminists, both Child and Fuller used the analogy between chattel slavery and the circumstances of a woman's life. Child's interest lay in the problem of female slaves and in the situations of southern white women who had to endure the sight of their husbands' mulatto children in the kitchen.[49] But Fuller used slavery to make the general connection between the institution of slavery and the condition of all women rather than dwelling on the sexual rivalry between a slave and her mistress or the slave's lack of protection: "As the friend of the negro assumes that one man cannot by right hold another in bondage, so should the friend of Woman assume that Man cannot by right lay even well-meant restrictions on Woman" (p. 37).

There was also a divergence in their opinions of Christianity's influence on the treatment of women. In general, Child believed that "Christianity, which has done so much for women—which, at a time when its pure maxims could produce nothing better, by reason of man's own evils, brought forth the generous spirit of chivalry from the iron despotism of the middle ages."[50] But when she compared the South Sea Islanders and the American Indians with "civilized" society, she wondered if Christian nations were as just as the Indians' and the South Sea Islanders' because "eternal infamy" remained with the woman who had been deceived rather than with the man. Fuller, too, questioned the double standard of sexual morality and was bold in her view that Christianity had not improved conditions for women: "The Man habitually most narrow towards Woman will be flushed, as by the worst assault on Christianity, if you say it has made no improvement in her condition" (p. 48).

The evidence seems to indicate that Fuller used much of Child's scholarship as a basis from which to draw further conclusions. She was much more radical in developing the concepts at which Child at times only hinted and at others openly suggested. Her choice of famous women as models of conduct for others to emulate, originally written about by Child, gives further evidence that Fuller had assimilated and reshaped some of Child's ideas in order to promulgate her message.

Margaret Fuller's debt to the feminist writers was great, but she was more than a synthesizer because she modified ideas to suit her purposes. For example, all of these feminists deplored the social pressures that caused women to marry for money or to marry almost any man out of fear of being left an old maid. Nevertheless, they favored love matches. But Fuller's concept of marriage was the most exalted because it was a religious one.

Again Fuller took a different approach to the old argument about the relative intelligence of men and women. Anna Jameson had asserted that women were less intelligent than men: "The intellect of women bears the same relation to that of man as her physical organization—it is inferior in power, and different in kind."[51] Harriet Martineau disagreed with her stand: "That woman has power to represent her own interests, no one can deny till she has been tried."[52] Instead of arguing the issue directly, however, Fuller pointed out that society wasted woman's power of intuition, the "fine invisible links" that connected the forms of life around them (p. 103).

When Margaret Fuller specifically mentioned the feminist writers in *Woman*, it was to comment on the conduct of their lives as much as on their writing. She excused George Sand's behavior because of the narrowness of a woman's lot, and she excoriated Madame de Staël for her inability to forget she was a woman while at the same time she recognized her romantic appeal. She used Harriet Martineau as an example of the influence an old maid's mind can exert, and she praised the brave stands of Anna Jameson and Lydia Maria Child for their defense of outcast women. But she celebrated

Catharine Maria Sedgwick as her supreme illustration of the kind of life that a noble and independent character could bring to a woman. Fuller emphasized the lives of these women as much as what they wrote because she sought models to inspire her readers to believe in the possibility of a fuller and freer life.

As a young girl, Margaret Fuller had started searching for role models whom she could emulate. The available sources of inspiration were meager, but she used them as advantageously as she could. She even absorbed the conventions of feminist style—the traditional disclaimer that one does not wish to disrupt the social order—of reassurance followed by radical proposals. As with her use of all other sources, she adapted any ideas from the feminists that promulgated her philosophy. However, her use of feminist sources was but one aspect of her research. *Woman in the Nineteenth Century* shows that she knew great literature, and when examining it, she sought to interpret it from a woman's viewpoint. Comparison of her work with the other feminists' writing shows that Margaret Fuller was braver and broader in scope and in aspiration. What she sought to do with her exploration was to give it universality and, ultimately, to make it apply to men as well as to women.

## NOTES

1. *Corinne* starts out with the story of a beautiful and independent young heiress who defies her stepmother in England and leaves to live as she desires in Italy. This novel depicts her changing from a brilliant improvisatrice into a maudlin invalid wasting away for the lover who deserted her.

2. The note and two sonnets written by Elizabeth Barrett were included in the first edition, *Woman in the Nineteenth Century* (New York: Greeley & McElrath, 1845), pp. 63–64, but were deleted from the main text by Fuller's brother, Arthur, who edited the 1855 edition, *Woman in the Nineteenth Century, and Kindred Papers Relating to the Sphere, Condition and Duties, of Woman.* He added this material to an essay about George Sand which he included in part II, "Miscellanies."

3. George Sand, *Mauprat* (Boston: Roberts Brothers, 1893), preface.

4. Letter to Elizabeth Hoar from Paris, January 18, 1847, in *Margaret Fuller: American Romantic: A Selection from Her Writings and Correspondence,* ed. Perry Miller (Ithaca, N.Y.: Cornell University Press, 1970), p. 262.

5. Note Miller's comment, ibid., p. 260, in which he asserts Fuller "deliberately jeopardized her entire plea for female suffrage by citing George Sand's life as the triumphant example of female emancipation." Miller complains not only of her advocacy of George Sand which "invited public censure," but also of her admiration "for the licentious Madame de Stael" and her defense of Goethe.

6. Mrs. Jameson [Anna], *Winter Studies and Summer Rambles in Canada* (London: Saunders and Otley, 1838), vol. 1.

7. In a letter written to Caroline Sturgis on March 9, 1839, Fuller mentions writing to Jameson: "I did not ask Mrs. Jameson for anything except some local particulars. I still think her conduct ingenuous, but not so much so, since I now think her knowledge more scanty than I had supposed. . . . I do not wonder she thought it impertinent in an obscure stranger to propose doing what Mrs. Austen, whom she seems so much to admire, did not feel competent to undertake. I have learnt some matters of fact from her book which will be of use." *The Writings of Margaret Fuller*, ed. Mason Wade (New York: Viking Press, 1941), p. 554.

8. Mrs. Jameson [Anna], *Visits and Sketches at Home and Abroad, with Tales and Miscellanies now first collected, and a new edition of the "Diary of an Ennuyée"* (New York: Harper and Brothers, 1834), 2:100.

9. Later this title was changed to *Shakespeare's Heroines*. The new title more accurately describes the contents of the book, which Fuller referred to as "Women of Shakespeare."

10. Mrs. Jameson [Anna], *Memoirs of the Loves of the Poets: Biographical Sketches of Women Celebrated in Ancient and Modern Poetry* (1829; rpt., Boston: Houghton Mifflin, 1900), preface.

11. Mrs. Jameson [Anna], *Memoirs of Celebrated Female Sovereigns* (London: George Routledge and Sons, n.d.), preface.

12. Clara Thomas, *Love and Work Enough: The Life of Anna Jameson* (Toronto: University of Toronto Press, 1967), p. 112.

13. Anna Jameson, *Shakespeare's Heroines* (1832; rpt., London: George Bell & Sons, 1897), p. 3.

14. Jameson, *Winter Studies*, 1:112.

15. Ibid., p. 113.

16. Ibid., pp. 112–113.

17. *Memoirs of Margaret Fuller Ossoli*, ed. Ralph Waldo Emerson, William Henry Channing, and James Freeman Clarke (Boston: Phillips, Sampson, and Company, 1852), 2:159.

18. See ibid., p. 160, in which Greeley commented: "Those who have read her 'Woman,' may remember some daring comparisons therein suggested between these Pariahs of society and large classes of their respectable

sisters; and that was no fitful expression,—no sudden outbreak,—but impelled by her most deliberate convictions." He added that if Margaret had been wealthy, she probably would have established a house of refuge for female outcasts. No doubt he was correct; she not only visited prostitutes in prison in New York but had them visit her. In a letter to James Nathan (June 24, 1845), Fuller mentioned visiting a house of asylum for released female convicts. She wrote: "I like them [prostitutes] better than most women I meet, because, if any good is left, it is so genuine, and they make no false pretensions, nor cling to shadows."

19. *Writings of Fuller*, p. 25.

20. Harriet Martineau, *Society in America*, 4th ed. (New York: Saunders and Otley, 1837), 1:148.

21. Ibid., pp. 148–154.

22. Ibid., 2:226–227.

23. Ibid., p. 227.

24. *Memoirs*, 1:191–194. This caused some coolness between the two women, although there was never a complete rupture in their relations, because she visited Martineau some years later in England.

25. Augusta Genevieve Violette, *Economic Feminism in American Literature Prior to 1848* (Orono, Maine: University Press, 1925), pp. 51–52.

26. Letter from John Neal, February 28, 1845, Fuller MSS., 11:117, Houghton Library, Harvard University.

27. See Mrs. Child's [Lydia], *The Mother's Book* (Boston: Carter and Hendee, 1831), p. 166: "Mothers urge upon them the necessity of getting married for respectability's sake. . . . I once heard a girl, accustomed to such remarks, say, with apparent sincerity, 'I should like of all things to be married, if I could be sure my husband would die in a fortnight; then I should avoid the *disgrace* of being an old maid, and get rid of the restraint and trouble of married life.' "

28. Seth Curtis Beach, *Daughters of the Puritans* (Boston: American Unitarian Association, 1907), pp. 28–29.

29. Catharine Maria Sedgwick, *Live and Let Live: or Domestic Service Illustrated* (New York: Harper & Brothers, 1837), p. 90.

30. Ibid., p. 79.

31. Ibid., p. 92.

32. Ibid., p. 87. Probably her source for this account was Lydia Maria Child's biography of Madame Roland, published in 1832.

33. Sedgwick, *Live and Let Live*, p. 72.

34. Ibid., p. 81. She uses public relations techniques by suggesting that mistresses should call their servants *domestics*.

35. Catharine Maria Sedgwick, *Means and Ends, or Self-training*, 2d ed. (New York: Harper & Bros., 1839), p. 269.

36. Ibid., pp. 268, 270.

37. Ibid., pp. 274–277.

38. Helene G. Baer, *The Heart Is Like Heaven: The Life of Lydia Maria Child* (Philadelphia: University of Pennsylvania Press, 1964), p. 183.

39. *Memoirs*, 1:55.

40. Mrs. Child [Lydia Maria], *Madame de Stael, Madame Roland* (n.p., 1832), p. 108. Child felt de Staël's defects were due to her lack of moderation: "everything in her character tended to extremes."

41. See Baer, *Heart Is Like Heaven*, p. 83, in which Baer says that Child "traced the history of women from ancient times onward in order to prove their equality with man."

42. Mrs. D. L. Child, *The History of the Condition of Women in Various Ages and Nations* (Boston: Otis, Broaders & Co., 1838), 1:72–74, 51–52, 2:163.

43. Each volume of ibid. contains 298 pages. Volume 1 describes women of Asia and Africa, and volume 2 is about the women of Europe, America, and the South Sea Islands.

44. Ibid., 2:213, 68.

45. As an editor of an abolitionist paper, Child never kept her place as a woman. In a review of *Woman* in the February 15, 1845, vol. 1, no. 7, issue of the *Broadway Journal*, Child writes: "This extending murmur of the human heart, this increasing conviction that woman should be the friend, the companion, the real partner of man in all his pursuits, rather than the mere ornament of his parlor, or the servant of his senses, cannot be silenced." Some years later in a note thanking George Curtis for his woman's rights speeches, she writes: "I thank you, in the name of the crippled class to which I belong, for trying to ennable us to walk without crutches. My disabilities as a woman have annoyed me more than I have told of." Baer, *Heart Is Like Heaven*, p. 292.

46. Child, *History*, 2:210–211.

47. Mrs. Child [Lydia Maria], *An Appeal in Favor of That Class of Americans Called Africans* (Boston: Allen and Ticknor, 1833). Publication of this work advocating abolition of slavery jeopardized the sale of Child's fiction. In her preface she explained her reason of conscience for writing her appeal, and she postulated the arguments in advance that will be said about her sex: "Read it, from sheer curiosity to see what a woman (who had much better attend to her household concerns) will say upon such a subject." She appeared to agree with the argument about a woman's concerns and then continued with her polemic. It is characteristic of her literary method on

occasions not to argue but to agree, and then to continue with her crusade "for truth and justice," which she would not exchange for "Rothchild's wealth, or Sir Walter's fame."

48. Child, *History*, 2:269.

49. *The Oasis*, ed. Mrs. Child [Lydia Maria] (Boston: Allen and Ticknor, 1834), p. 199. Child wrote: "Slavery is a poisonous and deadly vine twining about the sanctuary of domestic life. The unnatural and embarrassing relation that so often exists between their slaves and their husbands, their brothers, and their sons, is a sufficient argument against the brutal and degrading system. There is no denying this; the fact is proved on the very *face* of it."

50. Child, *History*, 2:210.

51. Jameson, *Shakespeare's Heroines*, p. 31.

52. Martineau, *Society in America*, 1:153.

# Chapter 4 Transcendentalism

Although *Woman in the Nineteenth Century* develops many of the issues that the feminists raised, the influence separating it from other feminist works is that of transcendentalism. In *Transcendentalism in New England*, Octavius Brooks Frothingham depicted the major philosophic concepts that are generally considered hallmarks of transcendentalism. After acknowledging that its roots were in ancient, Eastern, and Western metaphysics, Frothingham found its immediate origin in Immanuel Kant's *Critique of Pure Reason*. Kant used the term *transcendent* to "designate qualities that lie outside of all 'experience,' that cannot be brought within the recognized formularies of thought, cannot be reached either by observation or reflection, or explained as the consequences of any discoverable antecedents."[1] In opposition to John Locke's empiricism, Kant, Frothingham wrote, perceiving the "confusion that resulted from making man a satellite of the external world, resolved to try the effect of placing him in the position of central sway." Transcendentalism is a philosophy built upon universal principles, primary laws of mind, that are the ground of absolute truth. Using Kant's words, Frothingham explained that all cognition is transcendental " 'which concerns itself not so much with objects, as with our mode of cognition of objects so far as this may be possible *a priori*. A system of such conceptions would be called transcendental

Philosophy.' "[2] Also holding a position in opposition to Locke's, Theodore Parker wrote that the transcendental school maintained that "the mind is not a smooth tablet on which sensation writes its experience, but is a living principle which of itself originates ideas when the senses present the occasions; that, as there is a body with certain senses, so there is a soul or mind with certain powers which give the man sentiments and ideas."[3] A study of *Woman* indicates that Kantian epistemology is its philosophic foundation, as for example: "However disputed by many, however ignorantly used, or falsified by those who do receive it, the fact of an universal, unceasing revelation has been too clearly stated in words to be lost sight of in thought" (p. 19).

The transcendental movement in the United States developed some of its characteristics because of the religious climate at the time. It can be seen primarily as a religious demonstration. The descendants of the Puritans, having been emancipated by Unitarianism from New England's original Calvinism, found a new religious expression in forms derived from romantic literature, as well as from German philosophical idealism. George F. Whicher perceived transcendentalism as a revolt against materialism—that the "transcendentalists were deeply concerned with the quality of life in America."[4] Fuller in her acceptance of the spiritual nature of reality emphasized the importance of the individual soul as opposed to the masses and the forces of materialism. Moreover, throughout *Woman* she contended that a woman should live first for God, not for a man.

What happened next in the history of the movement is that transcendentalism, which began as a spiritual protest, "ended as an effort to reconstruct society on the basis of ideal laws and practical duties."[5] Theodore Parker, who saw the ethical nature of the transcendental movement, wrote:

> The problem of transcendental philosophy is no less than this, to revise the experience of mankind and try its teachings by the nature of mankind; to test ethics by conscience, science by reason; to try the creeds of the churches, the constitutions of the states by the constitution of the universe; to reverse what is wrong, supply what is wanting, and command the just.[6]

Henry Steele Commager has pointed out that many of the reformers of the transcendental era held a common belief in the perfectibility of man in the doctrine of progress. Therefore they could support Brook Farm or attend Fuller's conversations, despite the fact that she "was as dangerous as Fanny Wright."[7] Frothingham also recognized the reforming impulse that was characteristic of transcendentalism. He argued that the agitation for the enfranchisement of women, more definitely than any other reform movement, could trace its beginnings and the source of its inspiration to transcendentalism because "souls were of no sex." Fuller in *Woman*, Frothingham pointed out, based her claims on "rigorous fidelity to a philosophical idea; not passionately or hastily. Not as a demand of sentiment, not as a right under liberty, not as a conclusion from American institutions, but as the spiritual prerogative of the spiritual being."[8] With such an optimistic belief in the great possibilities of human nature, Fuller could admonish her readers to be perfect.

Another aspect of transcendentalism that is also characteristic of *Woman* is that it conveys a feeling of the excitement of the times. William Henry Channing best described this mood:

The summer of 1839 saw the full dawn of the Transcendental movement in New England. The rise of this enthusiasm was as mysterious as that of any form of revival; and only they who were of the faith could comprehend how bright was this morning-time of a new hope. . . . Transcendentalism, as viewed by its disciples, was a pilgrimage from the idolatrous world of creeds and rituals to the temple of the living God in the Soul.[9]

New England transcendentalism expressed the peculiarly American attributes of a sense of newness, the belief in infinite potentiality and in democracy: "Transcendentalism simply claimed for all men what Protestant Christianity claimed for its own elect." It could, therefore, assert "the inalienable worth of man; theoretically it was an assertion of the immanence of divinity in instinct, the transference of supernatural attributes to the natural constitution of mankind."[10] This, Frothingham explained, accounted for the philosophy's protean nature that could produce a philosopher, critic, moralist, or poet. Emerson characterized the spirit of the age in his 1841 lecture, "The Transcendentalist," in which he declared: "Our American literature and spiritual history are, we confess, in the optative mood; but whoso knows these seething brains, these admirable radicals, these unsocial worshippers, these talkers who talk the sun and moon away, will believe that this heresy cannot pass away without leaving its mark."[11] It is, then, this transcendental spirit or mood that is reflected throughout *Woman* and gives it what might be called its naive view of human nature or accounts for what could be considered its wishful thinking.

Ultimately the importance of the transcendental attitude or philosophy is that it gave birth to a literary movement, in which Fuller played a key role. She was as much influenced in her composition of *Woman* by her association with members of the transcendental circle as by what they wrote. It is not always possible to ascertain the extent of her debt. She knew German well and was the most important disseminator of European thought among the members of the Hedge Club, a name given to the transcendental circle, that met when Frederic Henry Hedge, a Bangor clergyman, was able to travel to Massachusetts. The informal meetings and intense interaction of this vital group make it difficult to pin down precisely the genesis of an idea.

Of all of the figures associated with the transcendental movement, no one else affected Margaret Fuller's thinking as much as Ralph Waldo Emerson did. As with the other transcendentalists, however, it is not always possible to tell who influenced whom. Letters are available that show it was Fuller who first sought an introduction. Despite the fact that she knew many prominent people in the Boston area, at the age of twenty-five she was still looking for, at the least, a mentor to instruct her, at best a prophet to inspire her, or a great person to emulate. The well-known description of his reaction to their first meeting is given by Emerson in the *Memoirs*. He was at first repelled by her mannerisms but later changed his mind after her aggressive campaign to win him. Descriptions of Fuller in a social situation show her as a kind of thespian whirlwind that carried her listeners along in the onrush of her verbiage. Holding her audience at all costs, she could mimic, be sarcastic, and then be melancholy in a quick change of mood. With these methods, she succeeded in getting the invitation she desired to visit Lidian and Ralph Waldo Emerson for three weeks in July 1836.

On this visit he read to her his *Nature*. The next year, in 1837, she heard him deliver his Phi Beta Kappa address, "The American Scholar," before a Harvard audience. At the beginning of their friendship, Fuller accepted Emerson as her mentor, but there were often times when they exchanged roles, especially when they discussed Goethe or other German romantics. Their intensely close friendship became ambivalent. Hence their contacts had grown less frequent by 1845, when she accepted a position in New York City with Horace Greeley's *New York Tribune*, an arrangement of which Emerson wrote Carlyle he did not approve.[12] Perhaps Caroline Healey Dall's description of Emerson's and Fuller's meeting at one of the evening conversations "like Pyramus and Thisbe, a blank wall between," is apt.[13] Society's wall was between them, but they both felt the compelling need to whisper through a chink in the wall.

*Nature*, Emerson's pivotal work, expresses both a search for and the means of attaining insight. Appearing in 1836, Emerson's "personal statement of his newly formed 'First Philosophy' served as a focus for the intellectual ferment of the Transcendentalist group as a whole."[14] Calling for freedom from traditional "dry bones of the past," *Nature* demands "new men, new thoughts," as well as "our own works and laws and worship." "The American Scholar" confidently proclaims that the "day of dependence, our long apprenticeship to the learning of other lands, draws to a close."[15] Often called our intellectual declaration of independence, "The American Scholar" was a challenge to the academic world. So, too, is *Woman in the Nineteenth Century* a declaration of independence from the customs of the past: "It is love that has caused this,—love for many incarcerated souls, that might be freed, could the idea of religious self-dependence be established in them, could the weakening habit of dependence on others be broken up" (p. 118). It is a manifesto that women should be independent of men: "It is therefore that I would have Woman lay aside all thought, such as she habitually cherishes, of being taught and led by men" (p. 119). Therefore, Fuller, perhaps inspired by the boldness of *Nature* and

"The American Scholar," asserted independence from the dead forms of the past.

Just as Fuller had absorbed some of the intellectual fervor and the calls for change that Emerson demanded, she also partook of the prophetic mode of Goethe, the English romantics, and the transcedentalists, proclaiming that a new and better age was coming. Just as she had labeled Fourier, Goethe, and Swedenborg as the prophets of the coming age, so, too, did her voice in *Woman* take on the tone of the prophet predicting a brighter age that inevitably must come, reminiscent of the optimistic prophecy of *Nature* and "The American Scholar." Emerson saw the recurrence of great prophets as highly significant. In *Nature* he listed Pythagoras, Plato, Bacon, Leibnitz, and Swedenborg as important prophets, whereas in "The American Scholar" he confidently asked: "Who can doubt that poetry will revive and lead in a new age?" Similarly, Fuller assumed the prophetic mode of confidence: "Yet, no doubt, a new manifestation is at hand, a new hour in the day of Man" (p. 20).

Although Emerson became increasingly concerned about American materialism, at first he foresaw the rich promise of American democracy. This confident belief in America is expressed in "The American Scholar": "It is for you to know all, it is for you to dare all. Mr. President and Gentlemen, this confidence in the unsearched might of man, belongs by all motives, by all prophecy, by all preparation, to the American Scholar. We have listened too long to the courtly muses of Europe."[16] Fuller, too, proclaimed confidence in America's potential. In tune with new Adamic thinking, she proclaimed: "This country is as surely destined to elucidate a great moral law, as Europe was to promote the mental culture of Man" (p. 25). Furthermore, she thought that in some respects American women had an advantage over European women because fewer traditions had developed in the United States. She had integrated this idea with Emerson's concept that "every man's condition is a solution in hieroglyphic to those inquiries he would put," when she wrote:

> But they [American women] have time to think, and no traditions chain them, and few conventionalities, compared with what must be met in other nations. There is no reason why they should not discover that the secrets of nature are open,

the revelations of the spirit waiting, for whoever will seek
them. When the mind is once awakened to this consciousness,
it will not be restrained by the habits of the past, but fly to seek
the seeds of a heavenly future. [P. 109]

Her belief that the individual apprehends God's truth through his
intuition was one to which Emerson again and again lent his voice:
"There are the voices which we hear in solitude, but they grow faint
and inaudible as we enter into the world."[17] Fuller reiterated her
acceptance of intuitive knowledge as the best basis to apprehend
truth for those who are receptive: "For the truths, which visit the
minds of careless men only in fitful gleams, shine with radiant
clearness into those of the poet, the priest, and the artist" (p. 51).

Listening to the promptings of their intuition leads some people
on some occasions to have a mystical experience, as Emerson described it in his famous quotation from *Nature*: "The currents of the
Universal Being circulate through me; I am part or particle of God."
Fuller, too, used the experience of mysticism to promulgate her
thesis: "Mysticism, which may be defined as the brooding soul of
the world, cannot fail of its oracular promise as to Woman" (p. 102).
The effect, therefore, of taking the role of inspired prophet is to
appear to give divine sanction to whatever views the writer is advocating. This attitude gives the work an aura of revelation, which
can be effective with the true believer but unconvincing to one who
does not subscribe to this type of religious philosophy.

Another Emersonian dictum that Fuller accepted as a means to
remake society was the importance of individual character. In his
philosophy of history lecture on March 2, 1837, Emerson delivered
his concluding address of the series with reflections on the individual man: "All philosophy, all theory, all hope are defeated when
applied to society. There is in it an inconvertible brute force and it is
not for the society of any actual present moment that is now or ever
shall be, that we can hope or augur well. Progress is not for society.
Progress belongs to the Individual."[18] Fuller took a similar position
with her attack, not on the educational establishment but on the
individual. She wrote, referring to herself:

This author, beginning like the many in assault upon bad
institutions, and external ills, yet deepening the experience

through comparative freedom, sees at last that the only
efficient remedy must come from individual character.
These bad institutions, indeed, it may always be replied,
prevent individuals from forming good character, therefore
we must remove them. Agreed; yet keep steadily the higher
aim in view. Could you clear away all the bad forms of society,
it is in vain, unless the individual begin to be ready for better.
[P. 76]

With a strong emphasis on individualism, Emerson, like others in
the transcendental movement, felt that each person was unique and
must look within his own soul to discover his peculiar contribution:
"Is it not the chief disgrace in the world, not to be an unit;—not to be
reckoned one character;—not to yield that peculiar fruit which each
man was created to bear."[19] Fuller used this concept of the
individual's uniqueness in her rebuttal to the argument that men
were able to protect women, especially when they loved them and
presumably had their best interests in mind: "But men do *not* look at
both sides, and women must leave off asking them and being
influenced by them, but retire within themselves, and explore the
ground-work of life till they find their peculiar secret" (p. 121).
Then after having retired within the self to find one's peculiar
secret, one must henceforth put one's faith in one's self. This view of
the virtue of self-reliance was one of Emerson's most famous ideas
and still is popular today. He clearly stated his belief in his address,
"Education," delivered at Providence, Rhode Island, on the occasion of the opening of the Greene Street School.[20] Emerson spoke on
June 10, 1837, at the time Fuller was first joining the school as a
teacher:

The great object of education should be commensurate with
the object of life. It should be a moral one; to teach self-trust; to
inspire the youthful man with an interest in himself; with a
curiosity touching his own nature; to acquaint him with the
resources of his mind and to teach him that there is all his
strength and to inflame him with a piety towards the Grand
Mind in which he lives. Thus would education conspire with
the Divine Providence.[21]

In "Self-Reliance," he continued with the same theme: "It is easy to see that a greater self-reliance must work a revolution in all the offices and relations of men; in their religion; in their education; in their pursuits; their modes of living; their association; in their property; in their speculative views." Again in this essay Emerson compressed his idea into one of his famous aphorisms: "No law can be sacred to me but that of my nature." Emerson's concept of self-reliance is reiterated throughout *Woman*, both in its broader aspect that all women should be independent of men and individually that each woman must rely on herself: "I have urged upon the sex self-subsistence in its two forms of self-reliance and self-impulse, because I believe them to be the needed means of the present juncture" (p. 175). Earlier in *Woman* she illustrated this concept with her persona, Miranda, who was permitted by her father to develop self-reliance: "This self-dependence, which was honored in me, is deprecated as a fault in most women. They are taught to learn their rule from without, not to unfold it from within" (p. 40). Thus Fuller pointed out that social customs and education normally prevented a woman from depending upon herself. This idea became a major motif: society did not permit women to unfold, much less to follow their own instincts, but the individual woman, despite all opposition, must make herself strong enough to do so. In effect, Fuller advocated Emerson's dictum: "Whoso would be a man, must be a nonconformist." She, of course, interpreted *man* as *person*.

Emerson held an exalted view of marriage when he was courting Ellen Tucker. At that time he had preached a sermon on love. With a view that is typically platonic, he had held that it is not the body but the spiritual properties that are loved. The affections tended to expect perfection in the loved one, and "from seeking perfection in the human friend were led to seek it in God."[22] After he had been married for the second time, he gave a similar though more subdued version of platonic love in his lecture on January 26, 1837, at the Masonic Temple in Boston:

> Let the husband and wife mourn for the rapid ebb of inclination, not one moment; yield it no tear. As this cloud-scenery fades forever, the solid mountain chains whereupon the sky rests in the far perspective of the soul, begin to appear. . . . No

word of kindness, no act of honor ever fell unpraised or un-
fruitful in this society. Patiently, slowly, it bore praise and
honor: provokes the like in the other party, and exalts the
connexion from year to year from a bond of nature into a bond
of souls.[23]

Fuller's ideal of marriage—that its basis must be spiritual rather
than physical—was similar. She wrote at some length of various
marriages through the ages from Dante's loveless marriage to modern society's doubt as to whether the "earthly bond must be a
meeting of souls, or only supposes a contract of convenience and
utility" (p. 70). Even when discussing the concept of equality between husband and wife, she appended the adjective *religious* to
recognition of equality and considered the highest grade of marriage
as a "pilgrimage toward a common shrine" (pp. 80–81).

When Emerson discussed marriage at the time he and Fuller were
most intimate, he categorized attributes characteristic of men and of
women, which she later used and modified in *Woman*. Emerson said
in his early lecture of 1837:

The first Society of Nature is that of Marriage, not only
prepared in the distinction of Sex, but in the different tastes
and genius of Man and Woman. This society has its own end
which is an integrity of human nature by the union of its two
great parts, Intellect and Affection. For, of Man the predominant power is Intellect; of Woman, the predominant power is
Affection. One mainly seeks Truth, whose effect is Power.
The other delights in Goodness, whose effect is Love. This
end is illustrated in the habits of that society. The man goes
abroad, and works in the world. The woman stays at home,
and draws him to his place. The man loves and collects the
useful. The woman decorates the house with the pleasant and
beautiful. The man loves solidity; the woman loves form and
order. The man, freedom; the woman, society. The man,
plain dealing; the woman, kindness. Such is the society which
the Divine Spirit institutes for the reproduction of man; and
the Rank of woman is always a measure of the civilization of a
state.[24]

With some qualification, Fuller accepted Emerson's categories as to dominant masculine and feminine attributes. She substituted, however, energy and harmony for Emerson's truth and goodness. Moreover, her view of what constituted masculinity and femininity was more complex than Emerson's:

> The growth of Man is two-fold, masculine and feminine.
> So far as these two methods can be distinguished, they are so as
>
> Energy and Harmony;
> Power and Beauty;
> Intellect and Love;
> or by some such rude classification; for we have not language primitive and pure enough to express such ideas with precision.
> These two sides are supposed to be expressed in Man and Woman, that is, as the more and the less, for the faculties have not been given pure to either, but only in preponderance. There are also exceptions in great number, such as men of far more beauty than power, and the reverse. But, as a general rule, it seems to have been the intention to give a preponderance on the one side, that is called masculine, and on the other, one that is called feminine. [Pp. 169–170]

Another concept to which Fuller adhered was Swedenborg's theory of correspondence, which Sampson Reed promoted within transcendental circles. Emerson particularly admired Reed's thinking when he heard him while still a Harvard College student. Reed's exposition of Swedenborg's ideas explained the theory of correspondence: "As our desires become more and more concentrated to those objects which correspond to the peculiar organization of our minds, we shall have a foretaste of that which is coming, in those internal tendencies of which we are conscious."[25] In sermons that were later published, George Ripley also depicted Swedenborg's concept of the correspondence between the material and the spiritual world:

> The things that are seen, moreover, are dependent, in a great measure, upon our own souls. We have another instance, here,

of the relation between the visible and the invisible, and the subjection of the former to the latter. It is often said, I am aware, that the soul is dependent for its character and growth, on the external forms of matter, with which it is connected, and that it is greatly influenced by them is a fact, which no observer of human nature can deny; but it is no less true, that the outward universe is to a great degree, dependent upon our souls for its character and influence, and that by changes in our inward condition, a corresponding change is produced in the objects with which we are surrounded.[26]

Emerson used the concept of correspondence in *Nature* but expressed it more poetically: "Build, therefore, your own world. As fast as you conform your life to the pure idea in your mind, that will unfold its great proportions. A correspondent revolution in things will attend the influx of the spirit." Fuller reshaped the concept of correspondence to a human level after discussing masculine and feminine attributes, but there was still a glimmering residue of the Swedenborgian meaning: "There cannot be a doubt that, if these two developments were in perfect harmony, they would correspond to and fulfil one another, like hemispheres, or the tenor and bass in music" (p. 170).

Fuller used the principle of undulation, to which Emerson gave eloquent utterance in "The American Scholar": "That great principle of Undulation in nature, that shows itself in the inspiring and expiring of the breath; in desire and satiety; in the ebb and flow of the sea, in day and night, in heat and cold, and as yet more deeply ingrained in every atom and every fluid, is known to us under the name of Polarity."[27] Fuller refashioned the principle of undulation in nature and then, as with the theory of correspondence, applied it to human nature: "But, as human nature goes not straight forward but by excessive action and then reaction in an undulated course, he misunderstood and abused his advantages, and became her temporal master instead of her spiritual sire" (p. 170).

In addition, Fuller strengthened her position with the romantic view of the need of the individual for growth. The English romantic poets had promulgated the possibilities for growth of the individual mind as one of their fundamental themes. The transcendentalists adopted this idea and applied it to a belief in the individual's ability to serve as his own conduit to the divine forces. Sampson Reed expressed this view in his *Observations on the Growth of the Mind*: "The mind must grow, not from external accretion, but from an internal principle." Fuller expressed this principle as a law: "It is not Woman, but the law of right, the law of growth, that speaks in us, and demands the perfection of each being in its kind—apple as apple, Woman as Woman" (p. 177). Accordingly what developed was an individual formulation of law. From the "law of nature," Emerson derived the "law of spirit." Using these principles, Fuller derived the "law of right," which to her was tantamount to the "law of growth," in her fight for women's rights.

In the relationship of Ralph Waldo Emerson and Margaret Fuller, there is, ironically enough, a parallel between Emerson's reaction to his disciple and that of Andrews Norton to Emerson. Although Emerson did not react with the public rage that Norton did when he replied to Emerson's "Divinity School Address" by way of the *Boston Daily Advertiser*, he did react with a form of passive resistance. Although Emerson first published "The Great Lawsuit" when he had replaced Fuller as editor of the *Dial*, he declined to write the preface for its enlargement, *Woman*, although he had originally promised to do so.[28]

But as his disciple, Fuller used all of the arguments that Emerson promulgated about the individual and applied them to women.[29] He assumed the role of a prophet to talk about the state of society, so she adopted it to prophesy a better era for women. He spoke of American democracy, so she pointed out that few men, and no women, had had a fair chance. Emerson said that through his intuition an individual must look within himself to discover his peculiar fruit, so Fuller looked within her own soul to hear a voice crying out for the expansion of opportunities for women. Emerson said to rely on the self because nothing could bring one peace but oneself; Fuller said she had been brought up to be self-dependent but that society considered that quality a fault in women. When Emerson spoke sentimentally of platonic love, Fuller demanded high standards of chastity and pure love from both men and women. After he urged his adherents to build their own worlds and charged that inaction is cowardice, she acted on her principles and wrote an elevated plea for women's rights.

In all of the transcendental metaphor, whether it were a recognition of the concept of correspondence or nature's principle of undulation, Fuller perceived a metaphor of the injustice of society to women and transformed these metaphors into her plea for a woman's independence to grow. What happened in the Emerson-Fuller relationship is that Emerson unleashed more forces than he had intended. His disciple had taken his message to heart. As Emerson described the transcendental movement years later, he said it was the time when the young men were born with knives in their brains. What he did not say, though, was that a young woman was also born with a knife in her brain, and he did not know what to do with her. As with his Unitarian predecessors, he had set in motion revolutionary ideas over which he lost control, despite the fact that he fought back. Whether Emerson could accept the implications of his optimistic vision of mankind is still at issue today, but Fuller, at the time she wrote *Woman*, was enough of a transcendental optimist to believe that men would recognize that a woman wished to learn the secret of the universe, with God alone as her guide and judge.

Unlike Emerson, the people who sympathized with Fuller's aspirations were the women who first supported her famous conversations. It is quite likely that many ideas later promulgated in *Woman* were first explored in Fuller's conversation classes. They began in Boston on November 6, 1839, and continued in a series until 1844, when Fuller left for New York to work for the daily *New York Tribune*. Although Elizabeth Peabody had held conferences for women as early as 1833, Fuller's conversations are generally considered by scholars to have served as a nucleus of the women's clubs and conventions that developed soon afterward.[30] This conclusion is warranted because ladies prominent in Boston society and married to influential men, many of whom were notable in the transcendental movement, participated in her conversations. These women included Mrs. George Bancroft, Mrs. Barlow, Mrs. Lydia Maria Child, Miss Mary Channing, Miss Sarah Clarke, Mrs. R. W.

Emerson, Mrs. Farrar, Miss Howes, Miss E. Hoar, Mrs. E. G. Loring, Mrs. Horace Mann, Mrs. Theodore Parker, Miss E. P. Peabody, Miss S. Peabody, Mrs. George Ripley, and Mrs. S. G. Ward, as well as others less known today.[31]

Although some mixed classes were held later on, Fuller designed the conversations for women. She declared in the autumn of 1839 her wish that they be held for well-educated and thinking women—for both mature women in need of stimulation and cheer and younger women who could state their doubts and difficulties in order to be helped by the experiences of others. Her aim for the conversations, Fuller wrote, was "to systemize thought, and give a precision and clearness in which our sex are so deficient, chiefly, I think, because they have so few inducements to test and classify what they receive. To ascertain what pursuits are best suited to us, in our time and state of society, and how we may make best use of our means for building up the life of thought upon the life of action."[32] These aims were later developed in *Woman in the Nineteenth Century*.

Comments from members of the class no doubt helped her to expand and to crystallize her own ideas that she later used in *Woman*. Her class procedure was recorded by Caroline Healey, who took notes as a young woman while attending the conversations. Healey studied Margaret's face, observing that it was "full of the marks of pain. Young as I am, I feel old when I look at her." Fuller began the discussions and then, by asking provocative questions, encouraged other members to participate. She especially respected the minds of young women, for "in no way was Margaret's supremacy so evident." In her discussions of mythology, Fuller stressed the power of female deities in the ancient world.[33] Other subjects discussed included fine arts, ethics, health, influences on woman (subdivided into topics on the family, the school, the church, society, and literature), as well as "Persons Who Never Awake to Life in This World," mistakes, faith, creeds, woman, demonology, influence, Catholicism, the ideal, war, Goethe, Spinoza, Bonaparte, vanity, prudence, and education. The interchange of the ideas with so many of Boston's intelligent women helped to give Fuller the impetus to write *Woman*. She discovered that she was not alone in her views, that the frustrations society imposed on women were vexing to others, and that by writing about this question, she would be able to reach an even larger audience than with her conversations.

In addition, it must be remembered that the Hedge Club accepted women as members, notably Margaret Fuller, Elizabeth Peabody, and Sophia Dana Ripley. George Willis Cooke explained how important this club policy was in the woman's movement: "In the transcendental club women were for the first time in America put upon a footing of perfect intellectual equality with men."[34] William Henry Channing made this point clear concerning the way that male members at transcendental meetings treated Fuller: "Men,—superiors in years, fame and social position,—treated her more with the frankness due from equal to equal, than the half-condescending deference with which scholars are wont to adapt themselves to women. They did not talk down to her standard, nor translate their dialect into popular phrase, but trusted to her power of interpretation."[35] This policy lasted only during the time of the Hedge Club. The Town and Country Club that succeeded it, which was founded by Bronson Alcott in 1849, did not accept women members.[36]

Being accepted as an intellectual equal was important to Fuller and, in addition to his inspiring sermons, was one of the reasons why she admired the widely respected Dr. William Ellery Channing. In her tribute to Channing she made this point: "He regarded them [women] as souls, each of which had a destiny of its own, incalculable to other minds, and whose leading it must follow, guided by the light of a private conscience. . . . The young and unknown, the woman and the child all felt themselves regarded with an infinite expectation, from which there was no reaction to vulgar prejudice" (p. 112). When she taught in the Temple School in Boston, Fuller had read German—chiefly the works of De Wette and Herder—to Channing one night a week, so she had had ample opportunity to talk with him. In *Woman*, she said that due to the work of Harriet Martineau, Angelina Grimké, and Mrs. Jameson, Dr. Channing had been led to think of injustices done to women and had said he might write upon the subject (pp. 112–113).

Another major contribution of the transcendentalists that affected Fuller's thinking was the *Dial*, which in November 1839 she agreed to edit. (She edited the *Dial* during the time that she held her conversations, and several women who attended the classes wrote poems and essays for it.) The reason for the decision to found the publication was that members of the transcendental group did not believe any existing journal adequately represented their beliefs.[37] As William Henry Channing wrote, they felt the need to establish an organ to express "freer views than the conservative journals were ready to welcome." No clear editorial direction was given to her, but the prospectus, probably written by George Ripley, states:[38]

> The purpose of this work is to furnish a medium for the freest expression of thought on the questions which interest earnest minds in every community.
>
> It aims at the discussion of principles, rather than at the promotion of measures; and while it will not fail to examine the ideas which impel the leading movements of the present day, it will maintain an independent position with regard to them.
>
> The pages of this Journal will be filled by contributors, who possess little in common but the love of intellectual freedom, and the hope of social progress; who are united by sympathy of spirit, not by agreement in speculation; whose faith is in Divine Providence, rather than in human prescription; whose hearts are more in the future than in the past; and who trust the living soul rather than the dead letter. It will endeavor to promote the constant evolution of truth, not the petrifaction of opinion.[39]

The purpose of the magazine was broad enough to have covered the expectations of various members of the Hedge Club. Fuller outlined her expectations for the *Dial* in a letter written March 22, 1840, before the first issue came out: "We must not be sanguine as to the amount of talent which will be brought to bear on this publication. All concerned are rather indifferent, and there is no great promise for the present. We cannot show high culture, and I doubt about vigorous thought. But we shall manifest free action as far as it goes, and a high aim."[40] Nevertheless, Fuller worked long hours at the task of soliciting unpaid contributions to the journal for which many held high hopes.

No contributor to the *Dial* more adequately represented what the

general public believed a transcendentalist to be than Amos Bronson
Alcott. Fuller taught in Alcott's Temple School for the academic
year 1836–1837. She took notes for him on which he based a second
volume of his *Conversations with Children on the Gospels*, a work that
was shocking for its time because of its veiled references to sex and
unorthodox interpretation of Christianity. Of her performance as a
teacher, Alcott wrote after her death that, although she was an
assistant at the school, they were seldom there at the same hours, so
he did not see as much of her as he wished. In his journal he
observed: "If I might characterize her in a word I should say she was
a *diviner*—one of the Sibylline souls who read instinctively the mys-
teries of life and thought, and translate these in shining symbols to
those competent to apprehend them."[41] After the school collapsed,
she still saw him from time to time. Alcott's journal entry dated
November 2, 1839, records a visit she made when he permitted her
to read his diary from January to July of that year. Hence Fuller had
ample opportunity to be exposed to his ideas. His so-called Orphic
Sayings, published in the first issue of the *Dial* in July 1840, were
singled out for ridicule by the news media and journals.[42]

Despite the criticism and parody the Orphic sayings received,
Fuller published more in the January 1841 issue.[43] Although puzzling, they embody many of the transcendental concepts regarding
intuition, truth, beauty, and the like in a form suggestive of ancient
Oriental religious writings. Alcott's Saying XLVII, "Actual and
Ideal," is representative: "The actual and ideal are twins of one
mother, Reality, who failing to incarnate her conceptions in time,
meanwhile contents herself with admiring in each the complement
of the other, herself ignorant of both. Always are the divine Gemini
intertwined; Pan and Psyche, man and woman, the soul and
nature."[44] This saying suggests some of the concepts of dualism that
Fuller perceived and later developed in *Woman*: "Man partakes of the
feminine in the Apollo, Woman of the masculine as Minerva" (p.
116). Somewhat puzzling about the Alcott-Fuller relationship,
however, is her reference to Orphic Sayings in "The Great Lawsuit," published in the July 1843 issue of the *Dial:*

> Another attempt we will give, by an obscure observer of our
> own day and country, to draw some lines of the desired image.
> It was suggested by seeing the design of Crawford's Orpheus,

and connecting with the circumstances of the American, in his garret at Rome, making choice of this subject, that of Americans here at home showing such ambition to represent the character, by calling their prose and verse Orphic sayings, Orphics.[45]

In *Woman*, written over a year later, Fuller included the above quotation and then added: "We wish we could add that they have shown that musical apprehension of the progress of Nature through her ascending gradations which entitled them so to do, but their attempts are frigid, though sometimes grand; in their straining we are not warmed by the fire which fertilized the soil of Greece" (p. 22).

In addition to not finding Alcott's writing inspiring, Fuller may also have been annoyed with Alcott for his letter criticizing the *Dial*. When she was editor, she had written him that his "Days from a Diary" would have to be published in the April 1842 issue instead of the January one. Alcott's petulant reply was published without editorial comment in the April issue along with his "Days from a Diary." After half-suggesting that his article be withdrawn, he wrote:

> The Dial prefers a style of thought and diction, not mine; nor can I add to its popularity with its chosen readers. A fit organ for such as myself is not yet, but is to be. The times require a free speech, a wise, humane, and brave sincerity, unlike all examples in literature, of which the Dial is but the precursor. A few years more will give us all we desire—the people all they ask.[46]

Considering the conflict between the two transcendentalists as to the priority Alcott's work should have received, Fuller may well have been more attracted by his quixotic way of life than by his writing.

Because Orestes A. Brownson was one of the most socially radical members of the transcendentalist group and a person who prefigured Marxist theories in a kind of class warfare view of history, in which he envisioned the dominant sentiment of his age as that of social progress, it would be logical to infer that he was a major influence in Fuller's thinking, but this was not the case. For a short period of time, Brownson had been associated with Fanny Wright and Robert Dale Owen, helping them to promulgate their radical views, although he later wrote to the *Cayuga Patriot* attempting to exonerate himself from charges that he was an Owenite.[47] Brownson met Fanny Wright in the fall of 1829 when she lectured in Auburn, New York. For a few months, Brownson, who at the time was editing the *Gospel Advocate*, a Universalist paper, became corresponding editor of the *Free Enquirer*. Although Brownson had disavowed being an Owenite by the time of his connection with the transcendentalists and was to become a Roman Catholic convert, it is reasonable to conjecture that he would have discussed the feminist ideas of these radical social experimenters with members of the Hedge Club. Brownson was not very persuasive in the circle because he proposed in discussions regarding the *Dial* that they should write for his already established *Boston Quarterly Review* instead of founding another journal. This proposal was not acceptable to Margaret Fuller or Ralph Waldo Emerson. Nevertheless, the first issue of the *Dial* contained a favorable review by George Ripley of Brownson's writing. On the other hand, Brownson's appraisal of the first two numbers of the *Dial*, published in his *Boston Quarterly Review*, was not entirely favorable. After acknowledging its reputation and influence on American thought and literature, he turned to an ironic note, calling the editors "radicals . . . who would radicalize in kid gloves and satin slippers. The Dialists belong to the genus *cullotic*, and have no fellowship with your vulgar *sans-cullotic*." Probably Brownson's ironic humor struck to the heart of the matter because he and Fuller must not have liked each other. Perhaps she considered him unpolished, whereas from his comments, he must have thought her overrefined.

A writer with whose position Fuller did agree, however, was Sophia Dana Ripley. Of the articles published in the *Dial* when Fuller was editor, the only one that deals directly with the question of women's rights is by Ripley. Entitled "Woman," it appeared in the January 1841 issue two years before "The Great Lawsuit."[48] As the wife of George Ripley, Sophia Ripley was well prepared to write an article on the problems of women, for she took an active part in their communal experiment at Brook Farm, where she taught history and modern languages and at the same time performed the household drudgery. Ripley's essay, only four and a half pages long, suggests some arguments that Fuller later developed in her book. The main difference in their points of view is that Ripley's argument centered around the practical problems encountered by a married woman, whereas Fuller's thesis involved all women from a more idealistic stance. Ripley was also a much more compressed writer than Fuller, for she managed to include much, and suggest even more, in a short essay. She introduced her subject with a note of irony:

There have been no topics for the last two years, more generally talked of than woman, and "the sphere of woman." In society, everywhere we hear the same oft-repeated things said upon them by those who have little perception of the difficulties of the subject; and even the clergy have frequently flattered "the feebler sex," by proclaiming to them from the pulpit what lovely things they may become, if they will only be good, quiet, and gentle, attend exclusively to their domestic duties, and the cultivation of religious feelings, which the other sex very kindly relinquish to their inheritance. Such preaching is very popular![49]

After this ironic introduction aimed at the clergy, she attacked the poetic view of woman as being too idealistic for a woman caught "in the midst of wearing cares and perplexities." From this idea she quickly proceeded to attack the concept of "woman's sphere," which she denigrated by saying that no two people are the same but are determined by what is peculiar to each. After using a favorite word of the transcendentalists—*peculiar*—she argued that "religion belongs to them as beings, not as male and female." This, too, is the germ of an idea Fuller developed in *Woman*.

Ripley next contended that the commonly held belief that a woman can lead a contemplative life is wrong because a wife must make her husband comfortable, often at the sacrifice of her own leisure. A wife, she believed, was pursued by petty anxieties and harassed by care, which required as much strength to meet as a man needed in battle or in the political arena.

Ripley further wrote: "In our present state of society woman possesses not; she is under possession." Developing this topic, she said that a woman exchanged the opinions of her parents for those of her husband, thus spending her life in conforming to him, instead of molding herself to her own ideal. To her children she becomes an "upper" nurse, whereas the father is an oracle. Next she seemed to blame women for their weak resolution, much as Fuller did when she adopted her "frailty" epigraph from *Hamlet*. Ripley suggested a woman needed encouragement when she asked, "Why is she not encouraged to think and penetrate through externals to principles?" Perhaps Ripley is alluding to the words in the prospectus published in the first issue of the *Dial*. Then commenting directly upon a wife's relationship to her husband, Ripley said that she must not "lean, but attend on him as a watchful friend." A wife's individuality, she argued, "should be as precious to her as his love." She explained that during moments of crisis and times of meditation a person is always alone, but she conceded that a woman's "high vocation" is as a creator of a happy home. A wife, however, must not be degraded by drudgery. After calling for a stern life plan, she wrote: "Thought should be her atmosphere; books her food; friends her occasional solace." After asking for stoical equanimity in the face of both prosperity and adversity, she concluded her essay with a question: "Is this the ideal of a perfect woman, and if so, how does it differ from a perfect man?" Later Fuller was to echo this thought with her "Be ye perfect."

It seems reasonable to conjecture that Ripley's short essay, which Fuller accepted for publication in the *Dial*, raised some of the issues that had already been discussed in the conversation classes, because the "sphere of woman," Ripley wrote in her introductory sentence, had been talked of more than any other topic for the last two years. Both women refuted the single "sphere of woman" argument, but it should be emphasized that Ripley's essay is more practical than Fuller's despite the fact that Ripley adhered to the *Dial*'s dictum of defining principles rather than touching on specific reforms. Her tone is at times ironical, at times reflective of the common-sense wisdom of a wife who has kept house for her husband, whereas Fuller's tone is passionate and elevated.

In addition to assimilating and reshaping the ideas of contributors to the *Dial* such as those of Sophia Dana Ripley, Fuller also began to clarify her own ideas during her tenure as editor. Tending to pro-crastinate when she had a headache, she had considered herself a slow writer, but filling the pages of the *Dial* often meant that she had to do much of the writing herself in order to meet her publishing deadline. Therefore, she was forced to translate or write in haste. She often wrote pieces that seemed to reflect her own anxiety as to the proper role of a woman.

In Fuller's submissions to the *Dial*, which Bernard Rosenthal characterized as "the only real examples of literary experimentation that the journal saw in its four years of existence," she explored the nature of woman.[50] Combining her interest in the occult and the romantic, "Meta," published in the January 1841 issue, dealt with the subject in a sentimental way. Originally written by Fuller when she was twenty-three, it concerns the writer, Klopstock, who wrote to his dead wife, Meta, continually after her death. The work attempts to reconstruct Meta's life in the next world. It is no surprise to learn that Meta's guide is Petrarch's Laura. Back on earth, Meta appears before Klopstock, who kneels before her in awe: " 'Hast thou come, my adored,' said he, 'From the home of bliss to tell me that thou canst no longer love thy unworthy friend?' " Klopstock's question, typical of the style of this effusive and sentimental work, shows Fuller's early search for some kind of ideal lady. A woman who had inspired her husband to the extent that he wrote letters to her after her death appealed to Fuller's imagination. In *Woman*, she continued to express her search for an ideal woman.

An expression of the occult power of the female appeared in her story, "The Magnolia of Lake Pontchartrain," published in the same issue as "Meta." Also sentimental, it is an allegorical tale using southern flowers—the worth of the bloom of the magnolia as op-posed to the orange blossom. She wrote: "Secret, radiant, profound ever, and never to be known, was she; many forms indicate and none declare her. Like all such beings she was feminine. All the secret powers are 'Mothers.' There is but one paternal power."[51] Her fullest exploration of the feminine principle appeared in the next issue of the *Dial* with the publication of "Leila."[52] Fuller described her: "And the men called Leila mad, because they felt she made them so. But I, Leila, could look on thee;—to my restless spirit thou didst bring a kind of peace, for thou wert a bridge between me and the infinite; thou didst arrest the step, and the eye as the veil hanging before the Isis." Later she delineated Leila's dual function: "Leila, with wild hair scattered to the wind, bare and often bleeding feet, opiates and diving rods in each over-full hand, walked amid the habitations of mortals as a Genius, visited their consciences as a Demon."[53] Rosenthal considers "Leila" a "tale of psychological self-investigation" of an order attempted only by Fuller's contemporaries—Melville, Hawthorne, and Poe.[54]

By the time she had written *Woman*, she had further refined her concepts of the complex nature of woman, to which she had first given utterance in the *Dial*. In *Woman* she used the story of the Seeress of Prevorst to illustrate her belief in woman's special genius, which she thought was "electrical in movement, intuitive in function, spiritual in tendency" (p. 115). In contemporary society she felt that credence was given to the Minerva side of woman but not to the aspect of woman's nature represented by the Muse. In fact, in an idea similar to the one quoted from "Leila" that men call her mad, she wrote that a modern Cassandra who possessed the electrical, magnetic element was generally unhappy in society; she was misunderstood by men, and if she were married, her husband would despise her power and "torture her" so that she usually was ill (p. 104).

A story that Fuller translated from the French for the *Dial* concerns the dilemmas facing women artists. "Marie van Oosterwich" appeared in the last issue that Fuller edited, April 1842. Delving into the psychology of a woman in love, it is a lengthy account of a woman artist who fell in love with a profligate man who was not worthy of her love. Fuller's choice of this story to translate and publish in her final issue as editor of the *Dial* is significant because it shows a woman who had been a dedicated and successful artist until she fell in love. Always faithful, the heroine found the man she loved in the arms of a woman he said resembled her and who was willing to be his mistress. This discovery precipitated the artist's death. In her will Marie van Oosterwich bequeathed the faithless man a yearly stipend. Thoughtful to the end, she included a proviso in her will that he never be told who had left him the money. In her preoccupation with the proper role of woman, Fuller may have chosen to include a story that defined a woman's conflict between artistic achievement and her quest for an ideal love, because it was resolved only by death.

Although Fuller's interest in Goethe had begun long before her editorship of the *Dial*, it may well have served as the catalyst to force her to put many of her thoughts related to Goethe on paper, both as literary and as social criticism. In her study of Goethe, Fuller seemed to have found a modern depiction of the models of women and of the possibilities of the female principle that she had long sought and had found before only in a study of mythology. In the July 1841 issue of the *Dial*, Fuller wrote a long essay reviewing Goethe's life and major works. She noted: "Goethe always represents the highest principle in the feminine form. Woman is the Minerva, man the Mars." Because Fuller at one time planned to write a biography of Goethe and has been recognized as one of the early promulgators of the study of German writers in America, the obstacles she faced in popularizing Goethe were mostly concerned with his personal life.[55] Hence she found it necessary to defend both his liaison with Christiane Vulpius and his service at the court of Weimar in order to discuss his writing: "The excuse must be found in circumstances of his time and temperament, which made the character of man of the world and man of affairs more attractive to him than the children of nature can conceive it to be in the eyes of one who is capable of being a consecrated bard." After making excuses for Goethe's conduct, she commented on his major works, beginning with *The Sufferings of Young Werther*, a work she treated in a somewhat apologetic manner as a necessary step in the growth of Goethe's genius. In her discussion of *Faust*, she conceded that Goethe was not a "prophet poet" but a "poetic artist." Continuing, she wrote: "Faust contains the great idea of his life, as indeed there is but one great poetic idea possible to man—the progress of a soul through various forms of existence." In "Goethe" she considered both parts of *Faust*, seeing the second as the result of a life of partial accommodation when compared to Dante's larger sense in his "Paradiso." Of Goethe's other works, she believed that despite their "miraculous beauty of execution," they were chapters to his idea of the soul's progress. The need for the growth of an individual's soul was one of her main precepts in *Woman*, and Goethe must be acknowledged as one of her masters.[56]

In her discussion of Goethe's other works, such as *Wilhelm Meister's Apprenticeship and Wanderjahre* and *Iphigenia in Tauris*, Fuller tended to focus on the role of women. Beginning with Goethe's own life in her search for models, she cited the influence of the Duchess Amelia of Weimar upon her son, the grand duke, Karl August. Fuller wrote: "Of her Goethe was thinking when he wrote, 'The admirable woman is she who, if the husband dies, can be a father to the children.' " She applauded Goethe for painting life as it really is in *Wilhelm Meister* and showed that Wilhelm's interest in the stage was a result of his refusal to follow the tradition of his father merely for the sake of money or a standing in society. She then depicted the various women with whom Wilhelm comes in contact, beginning with the countess whose household reflects an elegant ambiance, next with Teresa in whom he sees the blessings of domestic peace and an adequate mind, followed by Natalia who possesses the same virtues as Teresa though with more wisdom. Fuller then interjected an allusion that probably was a reference to Emerson's Aunt Mary Moody in her search for an ideal woman: "A friend of mine says that his ideal of a friend is a worthy aunt, one who has the tenderness without the blindness of a mother, and takes the same charge of the child's mind as the mother of its body." But in Goethe's writing she found this role played by Natalia's uncle, who was his ideal wise man. Then she continued with her exploration of Goethe's use of a woman to symbolize the spirit of a scene. She cited Philina as a representation of degradation; Mignon, the divine muse; Aurelia, the desire for excitement; and Teresa, practical wisdom. Again, she mentioned Natalia, suggested by Mademoiselle von Klettenberg, whom Goethe knew in his youth. The culmination in Wilhelm's search is Macaria, who, he comes to discover, really belongs to the solar system. Although she considered Gretchen ultimately the redemptive spirit in *Faust*, and Ottilia's saintliness the via media heavenward in the *Elective Affinities*, Fuller praised Iphigenia at some length as Goethe's representation of the feminine principle at its highest—a self-reliant Iphigenia who obeys the promptings of her own soul to transform those around her.

Two years later, when "The Great Lawsuit" appeared, she employed substantially the same material as she had used in her earlier essay about Goethe. The next year while writing *Woman*, she

further embellished her Goethean material and added Swedenborg
and Fourier to this section, making them all prophets of the coming
age. First she mentioned the influence of the women in Goethe's
life, who had "supplied abundant suggestions to his mind, as to the
wants and possible excellences of Woman" (p. 125). This development of the biographical material in the *Dial* essay is used to support
the thesis of *Woman*. Again she named Margaret (Gretchen) as a
representative of the redeeming power in *Faust* and Iphigenia as the
"steadfast soul, to whom falsehood is more dreadful than any other
death" (p. 126). She continued with the catalog of women from
*Wilhelm Meister's Apprenticeship and Wanderjahre*—Mariana, Philina,
Mignon, Natalia, Teresa, and Macaria—as representative steps in
his upward path. The main differences in her feminist work from
her critical essay are that she apologized less for Goethe's life and
explicitly judged his aim as "satisfactory" in his expressions of
woman (p. 128). Interpreting and narrowing his ideas to her focus on
women, Fuller continued: "He aims at a pure self-subsistence, and a
free development of any powers with which they may be gifted by
nature as much for them as for men. They are units, addressed as
souls. Accordingly, the meeting between Man and Woman, as
represented by him, is equal and noble; and, if he does not depict
Marriage, he makes it possible" (p. 128). Goethe then was given high
praise by Fuller for his treatment of his fictional women characters.

In this issue of the *Dial* Fuller also included her article, "Bettine
Brentano and Her Friend Gunderode." This piece of writing contains her comments relative to the friendship of Bettine Brentano
and the Canoness Gunderode, as well as copies of some of their
letters to each other. (Bettine Brentano is notable because of her
exchange of letters with Goethe, published as *Goethe's Correspondence
with a Child*.) The account of the friendship between the two
women, which was broken by the suicide of Gunderode, is by
contemporary standards excessive and sentimental. Its importance
in relation to *Woman* is that Fuller explored the nature of a close
friendship between women, and she indicated her dissatisfaction
with the cultural interests of American girls. She wrote:

> And not only are these letters interesting as presenting this
> view of the interior of German life, and of an ideal relation
> realized, but the high state of culture in Germany which

presented to the thoughts of those women themes of poesy and philosophy as readily, as to the English or American girl come to the choice of a dress, the last concert or assembly, has made them expressions of the noblest aspirations, filled them with thoughts and oftentimes deep thoughts on the great subjects.

Fuller cast an envious eye at a society she believed held greater opportunities than the American for the cultural development of women.

In developing what Fuller felt Goethe's contribution to be, it seems desirable to point out that although Goethe shared some concerns with the transcendentalists, and indeed through Fuller may have helped to shape their thinking, Goethe is included in this chapter on transcendentalism primarily because of the *Dial*. It was the transcendentalists who provided this medium for Fuller to bring to light ideas that she had held in embryo form and that she later developed in *Woman*.

What makes *Woman* a unique feminist work is its revolutionary spiritualism. Other feminists, except for Fanny Wright, had at least given verbal recognition to the Supreme Being, but the transcendental view of the immanence of God within men and women is manifest in Fuller's thesis. She had caught the transcendental contagion of hope.

Margaret Fuller expressed a hope and an optimism in *Woman in the Nineteenth Century* that events caused her to modify in her later writing. *Woman* represents the culmination of her transcendental idealism. It came into being because of the peculiar excitement in the air, the great expectations among the transcendentalists that all things were possible, even female emancipation. It was a time in American intellectual history when people talked about the state of their souls with high seriousness. Because of this movement, Fuller was able to find paying guests at her conversations; and she was able to write a woman's rights manifesto and have it published in the *Dial* as a logical development from the ideas already published there. To some extent each member of the Hedge Club contributed to *Woman*—if in no other way than that the men accepted women as members. It cannot always be determined precisely who conceived of an idea first or who culled it from European sources, but the mutual reinforcement and encouragement that the members of this revolutionary movement gave to each other helped to make it possible for Fuller to write *Woman*. It is only by viewing *Woman in the Nineteenth Century* as a transcendental work that it can be understood. This accounts for what some readers consider its flaws, and what others consider its merits.

## NOTES

1. Octavius Brooks Frothingham, *Transcendentalism in New England: A History*, with an introduction by Sydney E. Ahlstrom (1876; rpt., Gloucester, Mass.: Peter Smith, 1965), p. 12.

2. Ibid., pp. 10, 13.

3. Theodore Parker, "Transcendentalism," in *The Transcendentalist Revolt against Materialism*, ed. George F. Whicher (Boston: D. C. Heath and Company, 1949), p. 76.

4. Whicher, *Transcendentalist Revolt*, p. v.

5. George Willis Cooke, *An Historical and Biographical Introduction to Accompany The Dial* (1902; rpt., New York: Russell & Russell, 1961), 1:39.

6. Parker, "Transcendentalism," p. 83.

7. Henry Steele Commager, "Theodore Parker" (1936), in Whicher, *Transcendentalist Revolt*, p. 85.

8. Frothingham, *Transcendentalism*, pp. 175–177.

9. *Memoirs of Margaret Fuller Ossoli*, ed. Ralph Waldo Emerson, William Henry Channing, and James Freeman Clarke (Boston: Phillips, Sampson, & Company, 1852), 2:12–13.

10. Frothingham, *Transcendentalism*, pp. 108, 136.

11. *The Collected Works of Ralph Waldo Emerson*, with introduction and notes by Robert E. Spiller (Cambridge: Belknap Press of Harvard University Press, 1971), 1:207–208.

12. *The Correspondence of Emerson and Carlyle*, ed. Joseph Slater (New York: Columbia University Press, 1964), p. 407. After citing the benefits of the job, Emerson wrote: "Still this employment is not satisfactory to me."

13. Caroline W. Healey [Dall], *Margaret and Her Friends* (Boston: Roberts Brothers, 1895), p. 13.

14. *Collected Works of Emerson*, p.xv.

15. Ibid., p. 52.

16. Ibid., p. 69.

17. "Self-Reliance," in *Essays by Ralph Waldo Emerson* (Boston: Houghton Mifflin, 1883), p. 51.

18. *The Early Lectures of Ralph Waldo Emerson*, ed. Stephen E. Whicher, Robert E. Spiller, and Wallace E. Williams (Cambridge: Belknap Press of Harvard University Press, 1964), 2:176.

19. *Collected Works of Emerson*, p. 69.

20. Emerson had replaced Alcott as the speaker; Alcott's controversial educational publications and practices had made him unpopular.

21. *Early Lectures*, 2:199.

22. Ralph L. Rusk, *The Life of Ralph Waldo Emerson* (New York: Charles Scribner's Sons, 1949), pp. 133–134.

23. *Early Lectures*, 2:103.

24. Ibid., p. 102.

25. Sampson Reed, *Observations on the Growth of the Mind* (1826), in Perry Miller, ed., *The Transcendentalists: An Anthology* (Cambridge: Harvard University Press, 1950), p. 58.

26. George Ripley, *Discourses on the Philosophy of Religion Addressed to Doubters Who Wish to Believe* (1836), in Miller, *Transcendentalists*, p. 136.

27. *Collected Works of Emerson*, p. 61.

28. See *The Journals and Miscellaneous Notebooks of Ralph Waldo Emerson*, ed. William H. Gilman, et. al. (Cambridge: Harvard University Press, 1960), 9:443–445, in which he debated the issues of the Woman's Convention" at Worcester. He did not like the idea of a convention, although he recognized problems with property. "Few women are sane," he wrote.

29. Gradually, Emerson began to modify his opposition to women's rights, partly due to the influence of his daughter, Ellen. Rusk, *Life of Emerson*, pp. 440–441.

30. See Mason Wade, *Margaret Fuller: Whetstone of Genius* (New York: Viking Press, 1940), p. 76. In order to attend, the women paid twenty dollars for a subscription of ten conversations. Wade pointed out how expensive this subscription was; a series of lyceum lectures cost only two dollars.

31. *Memoirs*, 1:338.

32. Ibid., p. 325.

33. Healy, *Margaret and Her Friends*, pp. 113, 13. Healey notes in her table of contents that Emerson's discussion of the conversations in the *Memoirs* was inaccurate; he stated there were only five conversations in the series on Greek mythology, whereas in fact there were ten, and that he did not remember how many he had attended.

34. Cooke, *Historical Introduction*, 1:29.

35. *Memoirs*, 2:18–19.

36. Odell Shepard wrote that much against Alcott's wish but "at Emerson's earnest request, women had been excluded," in *Pedlar's Progress: The Life of Bronson Alcott* (Boston: Little, Brown, 1937), p. 443.

37. See Bernard Rosenthal, "*The Dial*, Transcendentalism and Margaret Fuller," *English Language Notes* 8 (September 1970): 28-36. Rosenthal's comments on Fuller's editorship of the *Dial* stress her independence from Emerson. Rosenthal contends that Fuller's *Dial* reflected her intellectual interests rather than the views of the American transcendentalists.

38. Cooke, *Historical Introduction*, 1:68.

39. *The Dial: A Magazine for Literature, Philosophy, and Religion* (1840; rpt., New York: Russell & Russell, 1961).

40. *Memoirs*, 2:25.

41. *The Journals of Bronson Alcott*, ed. Odell Shepard (Boston: Little, Brown, 1938), p. 409.

42. Thomas Wentworth Higginson, *Margaret Fuller Ossoli* (Boston: Houghton Mifflin, 1887), p. 159.

43. See Joel Myerson's discussion: " 'In the Transcendental Emporium': Bronson Alcott's 'Orphic Sayings' in the *Dial*," *English Language Notes* 10 (September 1972): 31-38, in which he considers the Orphic Sayings so ludicrous that they served as a lightning rod for transcendentalists.

44. *Dial*, 1 (July 1840): 97.

45. *Dial*, 4 (July 1843): 6.

46. *Dial*, 2 (April 1842): 409.

47. Letter, November 4, 1972, to the author from Professor Daniel Barnes, who edited Brownson's letter, "An Edition of the Early Letters of Orestes Brownson" (Ph.D. diss., University of Kentucky, 1970).

48. When "The Great Lawsuit" was published, Sophia Ripley wrote Emerson that "Margaret's article is the cream of herself, a little rambling, but rich in all good things." *The Letters of Ralph Waldo Emerson*, ed. Ralph L. Rusk (New York: Columbia University Press, 1939), 3:183.

49. *Dial*, 1 (January 1841): 362.

50. Rosenthal, "*The Dial*," p. 35.

51. *Dial*, 1 (January 1841): 294, 304.

52. *Leila* is the title of a novel written by George Sand in 1833 concerning a woman's disappointments in love.

53. *Dial*, 1 (April 1841): 462-466.

54. Rosenthal, "*The Dial*," p. 35.

55. The first Ph.D. dissertation concerning Fuller was written at the University of Illinois by a Professor of German, Frederick Augustus Braun: "Margaret Fuller and Goethe," in 1910.

56. The need for individual growth was also a popular idea with the British romantic poets.

# Chapter 5 Genesis, form, tone, and rhetorical devices

The first impression a reader may get from a hasty perusal of Margaret Fuller's *Woman in the Nineteenth Century* is one of effusiveness and formlessness. Containing a display of erudition that is impressive, it is prolix, as was the work of many transcendentalists and other writers of the past century.[1] In the April 1845 issue of his *Quarterly Review*, Orestes Brownson observed that *Woman* has "neither beginning, middle, nor end, and may be read backwards as well as forwards." In his satire, Brownson expressed aspects of the organic living quality of the work, but he did not discern its form. In the midst of its verbosity, it is still possible to see more of a pattern in *Woman* than has been maintained. Its basic structure is that of the sermon, which is appropriate, because *Woman's* message is hortatory. Its complexity and apparent lack of form are due to its dual nature. Within the sermon framework, *Woman* partakes of the major characteristics of transcendental literary art. But before analyzing *Woman* as a literary work from the standpoint of form, tone, and use of rhetorical devices, it is necessary to examine its genesis. If a study can be made of its genesis from an early draft, then some insight may be obtained as to the way in which Fuller's ideas were developing and thus a clearer perception of her composition of *Woman* is possible.

*Woman* developed from "The Great Lawsuit.—Man *versus* Men;

Woman *versus* Women," which was published in the July 1843 issue
of the *Dial*, a year after Fuller had relinquished its editorship to
Emerson. In her preface to *Woman*, she explained that she had
prepared her expanded version for publication in compliance with
wishes expressed from many quarters. Then she discussed her
change of title. She conceded that the meaning of the original title is
puzzling—"it requires some thought to see what it means." Her
preference, she told her readers, was to retain the first title in her
enlargement, but she was dissuaded from doing so by friends.
Although awkward, her early biographer Higginson explained, the
original title was intended "to avert even the suspicion of awakening
antagonism between the sexes."[2] Nevertheless, this title does sound
antagonistic because it suggests court action. But why is the title
worded "man versus men" instead of "man versus woman," or vice
versa, which is the usual order in the battle of the sexes? Fuller's
intention was not to write a long history of woman's grievances
against the tyranny of the male sex. Instead she keynoted the griev-
ance of the individual man or woman whose aspirations were
thwarted by the multitude, or by himself or herself, from becoming
the developed soul he or she might become. She explained:

> I meant by that title to intimate the fact that, while it is the
> destiny of Man, in the course of the ages, to ascertain and
> fulfil the law of his being, so that his life shall be seen, as a
> whole,to be that of an angel or messenger, the action of
> prejudices and passions which attend, in the day, the growth
> of the individual, is continually obstructing the holy work that
> is to make the earth a part of heaven. By Man I mean both man
> and woman; these are the two halves of one thought. I lay no
> special stress on the welfare of either. I believe that the de-
> velopment of the one cannot be effected without that of the
> other.

She developed this concept in *Woman* by adding to "Lawsuit" her
dual epigraphs. Then, by rephrasing them, she made them applicable to men as well. What she had to say applied to both men and
women; her message was not ambivalent but hortatory, and its
significance, again referring to her original title, was "great."

It appears at first glance that *Woman* is much longer than "Lawsuit," but a line-by-line examination of the content indicates that the number of words per page in "Lawsuit" is much greater than that in *Woman*. The first 130 pages of the 179-page text of *Woman* are a close adaptation of the 47 pages of "Lawsuit." In most instances, Fuller used a verbatim transcription of "The Great Lawsuit" in *Woman*. Occasionally she changed a few words to clarify or modify the meaning of a sentence, but she did very little polishing of her original text. For example, in the original essay she wrote, "Is it not enough, cries the sorrowful trader," and in her second version (p. 28) she changed *sorrowful* to *irritated*. In the original version she wrote, "But our doubt is whether the heart does consent with the head, or only acquiesces its decrees." In the second version, she changed *acquiesces* to *obeys* and then added to her sentence, "with a passiveness that precludes the exercise of its natural powers, or a repugnance that turns sweet qualities to bitter, or a doubt that lays waste the fair occasions of life" (pp. 29–30). Another word changed to clarify meaning is *incessant*, which in *Woman* becomes *frequent*: "Shrink not from frequent error in this gradual, fragmentary state" (p. 19). She deleted a phrase or a sentence a few times, but mostly she developed and elaborated on points she had already made. In her discussion of property rights for widows, she said that the wife "inherits only a part of his fortune" and then inserted in her second version the phrase "often brought him by herself" after "fortune" (p. 31). In her treatment of illustratious old maids—"No one thinks of Michael Angelo's Persican Sibyl, or St. Theresa, or Tasso's Leonora, or the Greek Electra, as an old maid"—she added, "more than of Michael Angelo or Canova as old bachelors" (p. 99), in order to give her sentence and idea balance. Sometimes she added discussions of writers whom she had not included before, such as Charles Fourier and Walter Savage Landor. Furthermore, she tended to add capital letters and italics for emphasis and occasionally corrected punctuation.

There are forty-nine pages of new material. The portion she added contains the most daring subject matter in the book because much of it was contemporary application of her thesis. Her new material contained some frank discussions of sex; an example of an incompatible marriage: "I have known this man come to install himself in the chamber of a woman who loathed him, and say she

should never take food without his company" (p. 32); the double
standard of morality: "Let Sir Charles Grandison preach to his own
sex" (p. 151); the notorious trial of Amelia Norman; a mother's
sadness when she gives birth to a daughter; the father's kidnapping
of his own children as a means of coercing his wife; problems of older
women—a well-preserved woman at forty who is spoken of
"upholstery-wise" (p. 99); property rights for married women; and
her idea that ladies are responsible for rehabilitating prostitutes.
More trenchant social criticism was used to supplement her earlier
points: "Those who think the physical circumstances of Woman
would make a part in the affairs of national government unsuitable,
are by no means those who think it impossible for negresses to
endure field-work, even during pregnancy, or for sempstresses to go
through their killing labors" (p. 35). Also included in her enlargement was her remark about letting women be sea captains. Although
she added the ancient belief that a baby's body was inherited from
his mother and his soul from his father, in general her new material
contained less spiritual transcendentalism until the peroration.
Therefore the most controversial writing in *Woman* was that which
she added to "The Great Lawsuit."[3] The importance of the earlier
draft is that it gave Fuller the courage to treat inflammatory subject
matter. Because the reception of "The Great Lawsuit" was on the
whole favorable among the *Dial*'s small coterie of readers, she became more outspoken. One criticism she did receive about her
earlier draft, as she herself explained, was that she did not make her
"meaning sufficiently clear" (p. 168). Consequently, she may have
been guilty of repetition. And in order to make her meaning unmistakable, less of it is veiled in metaphor.

The residue of a trial from "The Great Lawsuit" remains. The
thinking man or woman, who has not yet become the enlarged soul
he or she would become, is admonished to perfect himself despite all
obstructions. Once this extraordinary person frees himself from
ordinary frailty, then this individual could become the king or
queen she seeks to lead and to inspire his waiting adversaries.

The broadest structural framework of *Woman* reflects the sermon,
which she mentioned both in her introduction—"sermons preached
from the text" (p. 19)—and in her statement in the conclusion that
she would retrace her design "as was done in old-fashioned ser-

mons" (p. 168). Closely akin to the sermon is the oration, and *Woman* contains elements of both forms. Fuller began her work with the classic exordium in a vague way so her thesis is not clear for several pages. Using caution, Latin and German quotations, and preliminary conciliation, she did not introduce her *propositio* until the tenth page: woman needs her turn, and improvement of her lot would aid in the reformation of men, too. Then she stated her sermon topic: "Be ye perfect." Having established her thesis at last, she proceeded with *partitio* or analysis of her subject, which is done in a debate style by raising the popular arguments men used with which to oppose women's rights, and then rebutting them. She began with the conversational method of questions and answers characteristic of the speaker who wishes to dramatize a point. A husband asks:

> "Is it not enough," cries the irritated trader, "that you have done all you could to break up the national union, and thus destroy the prosperity of our country, but now you must be trying to break up family union, to take my wife away from the cradle and the kitchen-hearth, to vote at polls, and preach from a pulpit? Of course, if she does such things, she cannot attend to those of her own sphere. She is happy enough as she is. She has more leisure than I have,—every means of improvement, every indulgence."
>
> "Have you asked her whether she was satisfied with these *indulgences*?"
>
> "No, but I know she is." [Pp. 28–29]

Fuller ended this dialogue by saying that liberating measures are proposed to ascertain truth. Objectively, she continued: "Without enrolling ourselves at once on either side, let us look upon the subject from the best point of view which to-day offers" (p. 31). She debated the issue with rebuttals that accelerated in strength until she concluded, "We would have every arbitrary barrier thrown down" (p. 37).

Then in a long *digressio* composed of sermon-style exemplar, she considered all that is known of woman, delineating her story in myth, folklore, the Bible, poetry, fiction, history, and in her own time. Beginning with an extensive analysis of the institution of marriage, she examined the life cycle of a woman. She sought women whose lives she found inspiring such as Queen Isabella of Castile, or Marina, the Indian woman who accompanied Cortez, but she evaluated the lives of other women, such as Queen Elizabeth and Mary Stuart, lauding their strengths and castigating their weaknesses. Interwoven in her examples is an attempt to buttress her argument with authority using the views of recognized authors to support her position. She conceded that women have always had some power, but they want freedom from men to learn the secrets of the universe alone. Within her narrative in a form suggestive of the *reprehensio* is admonition to men, who refuse to grant women freedom and who call strong women "manly," and to women, who misuse what power they have. Scornfully she recognized that a coquette, a shrew, or a good cook could have lifelong sway.

Fuller inculcated within her discussion a realistic assessment of the options open to women in various societies, ancient and modern. Reasonably enough, since most women would marry, she spent a lot of time examining the institution of marriage. She contrasted idealized concepts of courtly love in which the lady served as inspiration with the reality of arranged marriages of convenience. It is no surprise that she advocated not only a marriage of love but a spiritual union of two souls on a common pilgrimage. She also discussed other options women have, such as women who write, women who are mothers, and women who do not marry, as well as the problems of women in middle and old age. She praised women abolitionists brave enough to speak on the platform but warned that they must work for measures not only favoring slaves but also for themselves. In her all-inclusive discussion of a woman's life cycle, she discussed the child toward the end of this section, lamenting the father who stunts his daughter's education for fear she will not find a husband. Again pointing out that a woman must work alone and use her special gifts of intuition, she mentioned a crisis at hand and prophesied a new Jerusalem, which the prophets Swedenborg, Fourier, and Goethe foretell. Then her sermon became more direct as she preached about the problems of prostitutes and polygamy and warned that men must be as pure as women. In an accelerating evocative vision of the future in which both men and women rule their passions by reason, she placed her hope with the young—"harbingers and leaders of a new era" (p. 155). Triumphantly she concluded her long narrative by proclaiming her expectation that a young "Exaltada" would serve as an "example and instruction for the rest" (p. 156).

The structural pattern of *Woman* next takes the sermon form of an *applicatio* in a departure from the main thrust of the argument and moves from the visionary future to the prosaic present. Fuller sighed over books recently published in which the chief point was to fit a wife "to please, or, at least, not to disturb a husband" (p. 158). She recognized the dilemmas women faced and completed this section by admonishing American women to use their moral power and not to let themselves be intimidated by aspersions on their modesty. Her application of her sermon, therefore, is that women must act to save themselves (p. 168).

From practical application of the sermon, the form of *Woman* soars back to the sublime world of the spirit. In a peroration, Fuller outlined the major points of her argument and of her vision of the harmonious world that an ideal relationship between men and women would bring. Then, like a minister ending a sermon, she addressed a prayer to God: "Thou, Lord of Day!" After a cold winter, she prophesied a distant day of glory. With a final hortatory admonition to cherish hope and act, she concluded with poetry that echoed the Bible: "Persist to ask, and it will come." With an allusion to her epigraphs, she envisioned—"So shalt thou see, what few have seen,/ The palace home of King and Queen"—and thus gave structural and thematic wholeness to her work.

The structure of *Woman* does seem to fit loosely the sermon-oration form. What tends to obscure its pattern is Fuller's use of writing techniques derived from transcendentalism. According to precepts generally accepted by the transcendentalists, a work of literature grows out of experience and hence is organic. As Coleridge, a romantic, wrote: "The organic form is innate; it shapes, as it develops itself from within." And Keats, using a nature metaphor, explained that good poetry grew as naturally as the leaves on a tree. Emerson later used this concept, saying a poem is "a thought so passionate and alive that like the spirit of a plant or an animal it has an architecture of its own." The basic assumption of transcendental art is of the "superiority of the spirit to the letter." Art as inspiration meant that the word became one with the thing. Ultimately, the "transcendental theory of art is a theory of knowledge and religion as well." Hence transcendental expression must coalesce the seer and spectacle into one, an organic whole.[4] Margaret Fuller, the observer, united the spectacle—her experience—with that of all other women into the final fusion of *Woman in the Nineteenth Century*.

As early as 1826 Sampson Reed published his "Observations on the Growth of the Mind," setting forth transcendental literary theory. He wrote: "Syllogistic reasoning is passing away," leaving nothing behind but a demonstration "of its own worthlessness." Both Julia Ward Howe and Arthur W. Brown pointed out that there was no systematic parallelism in *Woman*; however, Fuller did not intend that there should be.[5] By not following a rigidly organized pattern of syllogistic reasoning, she was merely demonstrating that she had accepted the transcendentalist aesthetic theory that, as a member of the club, she had helped to shape. The movement of her treatise is not parallel but soaring and circular. Its dominant mode of composition is an unfolding from the subconscious in a form of spiraling thought patterns. One of her recurrent themes is an optimistic refrain that appears in a mood of confidence, disappears in a burst of admonition, and later reappears in a form of wavelike undulation characteristic of transcendental writing. Moreover, the polarities of optimistic expectation (symbolized by the epigraph, "The Earth waits for her Queen") and impatient anger (symbolized by, "Frailty, thy name is Woman") have an ebb and flow rhythm to them. She may begin in a lull with a mundane matter such as the problem of a poor widow whose husband has died leaving no will and accelerate in intensity to the sublime "ravishing harmony of the spheres," or start at the crest of the wave as it flows back to the sea. From practical application of her sermon, the thought patterns of *Woman* soar back to the world of the spirit. Instead of syllogistic reasoning, order comes from the authority that the certitude of intuition brings.

A characteristic of transcendental literature, which *Woman* reflects, is subjectivity—the individual as the center of the world. At times this method suggests a free association of ideas. One authority requires that another be included; one mythological figure suggests another. Ultimately the thought patterns lead from the conscious, to the subconscious mind, to the transcendental well-spring of truth, the divine intuition. Fuller used her own experience as representative of the experience of all women—that indeed the lot of woman is sad, that all women need and, in fact, should aspire to the same self-culture and fulfillment that she herself had desired. She began *Woman* by using the conventional "we" but she changed to "I" after only fifteen pages. Later she alternated between "we" and "I." She gave an account of her youthful education by her father under the guise of the persona, Miranda, as an example of an independent girl who was respected for being self-reliant. Fuller told this story by means of an imaginary conversation in which the "I" takes the role of the foil to Miranda's explanation of her youthful training in self-reliance, so unusual for a girl of that day (pp. 38–41). In her subjectivity there are times when she almost linked herself with the queen that the earth awaits. If not the queen directly, she associated herself in her description of Miranda with the woman of genius, possessor of the magnetic electrical element (intuition), who has a contribution to make to the world—"a strong electric nature, which repelled those who did not belong to her, and attracted those who did" (p. 39). At another time in the discussion of woman's power of intuition, she wrote: "Women who combine this organization with creative genius are very commonly unhappy at present. They see too much to act in conformity with those around them, and their quick impulses seem folly to those who do not discern the motives" (p. 103). By looking into her own soul, she saw reflected there the problems and the frustrated aspirations of other women: "but what concerns me now is, that my life be a beautiful, powerful, in a word, a complete life in its kind. Had I but one more moment to live I must wish the same" (p. 177). Starting from her own angle of vision, she unfolded her hopes to the world, and she concluded her treatise as a prophet:

> I stand in the sunny noon of life. Objects no longer glitter in the dews of morning, neither are yet softened by the shadows of evening. Every spot is seen, every chasm revealed. Climbing the dusty hill, some fair effigies that once stood for symbols of human destiny have been broken; those I still have with me show defects in this broad light. Yet enough is left, even by

experience, to point distinctly to the glories of that destiny;
faint, but not to be mistaken streaks of the future day. [P. 178]

Thus her subjectivity became universal as she linked her own experience to that of the experience of all women and prophesied that
in the future life would be better for them.

The tone of *Woman* reinforces the idea that Fuller was writing a
didactic work. At times the tone admonishes the audience to act; at
other times it is declamatory, but dominantly it is conversational.
Although its voice patterns are conversational, the archness of
Fuller's diction and tone is transcendental. Today, the mannerism
of Fuller's speaking style may sound affected. Nevertheless, many
people who knew Fuller said that her chief talent was as a speaker, so
it is not surprising that instead of syllogisms, many phrases contain
the emotive power of a conversation, of which she would have been
the star. Her writing technique included both questions and
answers in a debate form, but it also revealed the hallmark of the
accomplished conversationalist: a flair for the dramatic. At best her
conversational technique suggests breathless ejaculations rather
than sentences. In a kind of accelerating excitement, she used the
hortatory style: "Let us be wise, and not impede the soul. Let her
work as she will. Let us have one creative energy, one incessant
revelation. Let it take what form it will, and let us not bind it by the
past to man or woman, black or white. Jove sprang from Rhea,
Pallas from Jove. So let it be" (p. 117). Then her tone changes to one
of intimacy. Her writing sounds as if she were talking to a small
group and studying the reaction of her audience.

In the following passage, she revealed that she was a perceptive
performer who could quickly adapt an argument to match the mood
of her imaginary audience by modifying, explaining, and then
hammering home at the proper psychological moment the point she
intended to make in the first place:

If it has been the tendency of these remarks to call Woman
rather to the Minerva side,—if I, unlike the more generous
writer, have spoken from society no less than the soul,—let it
be pardoned! It is love that has caused this,—love for many
incarcerated souls, that might be freed, could the idea of

religious self-dependence be established in them, could the weakening habit of dependence on others be broken up. [P. 118]

Her excuse for her stand was love. In effect, she seemed to be anticipating objections. Her most famous suggestion combines a speaking conversational style with her flair for dramatization: "But if you ask me what offices they may fill, I reply—any. I do not care what case you put; let them be sea-captains, if you will" (p. 174). Her frequent use of dashes suggests the pause used by accomplished speakers.

Other passages in *Woman* combine the dramatic method of composition with an aphoristic technique: "Tremble not before the free man, but before the slave who has chains to break" (p. 63); "Whatever abuses are seen, the timid will suffer; the bold will protest" (p. 77). In her dramatization of her thesis, she used an aphoristic method of attracting attention by reversing sex roles, beginning with her suggestion that the time had come for "Eurydice to call for an Orpheus, rather than Orpheus for Eurydice" (p. 23).[6] Again she wrote: "Presently she [nature] will make a female Newton, and a male Syren" (p. 116). "But Penelope is no more meant for a baker or weaver solely, than Ulysses for a cattle-herd" (p. 44). Later she suggested, not unlike semantic changes in vogue today, that the title given to a party abroad, "Los Exaltados," be changed to "Los Exaltados, Las Exaltadas" (p. 156). This stylistic device of sex role reversal is used to advocate one of her central ideas—that there is no "wholly masculine man, no purely feminine woman" (p. 116)—which culminates in the "sea-captain" passage.

Whether that of a preacher, orator, or confidante, the tone of *Woman* expresses the spoken word. Hence many of Fuller's images relate to sound. Perhaps here she echoes Shelley, whom she admired: "And, if men are deaf, the angels hear. But men cannot be deaf" (p. 26). She used music as a means of expressing the divine: "Then their sweet singing shall not be from passionate impulse, but the lyrical overflow of a divine rapture, and a new music shall be evolved from this many-chorded world" (p. 121). Or she saw woman as a bird with clipped wings that desires to fly and sing: "no need to clip the wings of any bird that wants to soar and sing" (p.

175). That she frequently preferred sound imagery to that of sight is again indicated by her final poem:

> For the Power to whom we bow
> Has given its pledge that, if not now,
> They of pure and steadfast mind,
> By faith exalted, truth refined,
> *Shall* hear all music loud and clear,
> Whose first notes they ventured here. [Pp. 178–179]

Another type of rhetorical device that Fuller often used is imagery derived from organicism, which implies movement, growth, expansion, or fruition. Her argument rested on the "law of growth." She used phrases such as *ampler fruition*, *fruitful summer*, or *plants of great vigor will always struggle into blossom*. She liked movement related to the life force symbolized by the heart: "I must beat my own pulse true in the heart of the world; for *that* is virtue, excellence, health" (p. 178). And the cycles of nature—the flowing of streams, the waxing moon, and noon-morning-dawn imagery—are favorites.

Yet despite her frequent choice of auditory and organic imagery, her work's salient characteristic is its great use of references to literature, history, religion, and mythology. These references are used primarily as an exemplar for her readers to emulate, as recognized authority to support her topic, or as allusions to Holy Writ.

Since the structure of *Woman* is sermon-like, Fuller used biblical allusions as the major support for her near-rhapsodic religious vision of the great potentialities of men and women. She derived her thematic exhortation—"Be ye perfect"—from Matthew 5:48, from which she deleted "therefore." On occasion she quoted directly from the Bible: "This is the Law and the Prophets. Knock and it shall be opened; seek and ye shall find" (p. 19). Another way that she used biblical sources was to reshape a scriptural passage. Matthew 5:13 reads: "Ye are the light of the world. A city that is set on a hill cannot be hid. Neither do men light a candle, and put it under a bushel, but on a candlestick; and it giveth light unto all that are in the house." Fuller changed the meaning: "The candlestick set in a low place has given light as faithfully, where it was needed, as that upon the hill" (p. 17). In this passage, she incorporated biblical allusions and Christian concepts: "Love has already been expressed, that made all things new, that gave the worm its place and ministry as well as the eagle; a love to which it was alike to descend into the depths of hell, or to sit at the right hand of the Father" (p. 20). She used a clause such as *a love that cannot be crucified* or commonly used biblical terms as *future Eden, lamb, green pastures, Prince of Peace,* and *Holy Child* to symbolize hope and renewal. From traditional Christian theology she derived a reference to the deadly sin of sloth. Phrases that connote Calvinism, such as "doomed in future stages of his own being to deadly penance," can be found in *Woman*. Elements of the providential doctrine appear: "Yet, by men in this country, as by the Jews, when Moses was leading them to the promised land, everything has been done that inherited depravity could do, to hinder the promise of Heaven from its fulfillment" (p. 25).

She found inspiration in the figure of the Madonna, whom she mentioned several times: "No figure that has ever arisen to greet our eyes has been received with more fervent reverence than that of the Madonna" (p. 56). She referred to the Virgin Mary's powerful influence to reinforce her idea that women are born not only to nurture and alleviate the loneliness of men but also are possessors of immortal souls.

But it was to the Old Testament that she turned for the woman who would redeem mankind. Adam, she wrote somewhat ironically, "is not ashamed to write that he could be drawn from heaven by one beneath him,—one made, he says, from but a small part of himself" (p. 56). Adam "accuses" Woman—through her "Man was lost, so through woman must Man be redeemed" by "Immortal Eve" (p. 156).

Fuller employed biblical and religious allusions in the usual way to clarify meaning and as the wellsprings of her treatise. In addition, she cited contemporary writers—feminists, socialists, and transcendentalists—to buttress her argument that women could play a broader role in society. Her use of allusions to outstanding women from all recorded time, however, was complex. Their use is not an affectation but an intrinsic part of her way of thinking and the rhetorical method she adopted in order to make her point. Her allusions not only clarify her meaning but also serve as models of conduct to inspire or instruct women. Examples used as affirmations are taken from poetry, such as Britomart; from history, such as Aspasia; from mythology, such as Isis and Iduna or Sita in the *Ramayana*; from folklore, such as Cinderella; or from more contemporary life, such as the Polish Countess Emily Plater. Instead of cataloging lists of words, as Emerson suggested and Whitman did, her technique was to catalog women. She barely escaped creating an encyclopedic effect because she appears not to have wanted to leave anyone out. She admitted she "may have been guilty of much repetition" (p. 168). It could be argued that Fuller should have been more selective,[7] but on the other hand,[8] through sheer weight of numbers, the women cited from the ages become a catalog that is an evocation, a challenge to men to remove "arbitrary barriers" through proof that women can succeed. Thus she explained her use of her numerous examples: "I have aimed to show that no age was left entirely without a witness of the equality of the sexes in function, duty, and hope" (p. 172). As Fuller said, the function of her examples is to serve as a witness. Her citation of women from history and women from fiction finally blends into women from mythology. Her search led her to delve beyond patriarchal Hebrew-Christian society to the prototype mythic woman—an earth mother who was recognized as a powerful figure, a priestess with powers of intuition and serving as a medium to the divine. Fuller's figures become in themselves the incarnation of concepts. Cassandra and Iphigenia serve as witnesses to her argument that not only are women enslaved in Western civilization but that they are not allowed to use their special gifts of "electric or magnetic powers" with which they could be enriching the world. She cited the Seeress of Prevorst and "a friend" as examples of contemporary women whose gift of psychic power was wasted. Summarizing this concept, she asked: "Grant her, then, for a while, the armor and the javelin. Let her put from her the press of other minds, and meditate in virgin loneliness. The same idea shall reappear in due time as Muse, or Ceres, the all-kindly, patient Earth-Spirit" (p. 121). It was to classical mythology that Fuller turned for models to illustrate her ideas of the possibilities of the feminine principle.

In her search for an ideal of feminine virtue, she considered many of Shakespeare's heroines. She preferred his portrait of Cordelia, whose virtue she greatly admired. She also discussed the quality of

the marriages he portrayed and found the marriage of Portia and
Brutus superior to those in *Cymbeline* and *Othello*. Nevertheless, she
used the relationship between Portia and Brutus as an example of the
way women were neglected in ancient Rome. She thought Shakespeare was a genius with greater poetic power than John Ford and
Philip Massinger, whom she also cited, but believed he did not
portray women as heroic as they did or as did Spenser:

> Shakespeare's range is also great; but he has left out the heroic
> characters, such as the Macaria of Greece, the Britomart of
> Spenser. Ford and Massinger have, in this respect, soared to a
> higher flight of feeling than he. It was the holy and heroic
> Woman they most loved, and if they could not paint an Imogen,
> a Desdemona, a Rosalind, yet, in those of a stronger mould,
> they showed a higher ideal, though with so much less poetic
> power to embody it, than we see in Portia or Isabella. [Pp.
> 66–67]

Her main interest in her evaluation of Shakespeare's female characters was whether their images were heroic.

Of all of the authors in British literature, Fuller chose Edmund
Spenser as the one who gave the best portraits of female characters:
"The range of female character in Spenser alone might content us for
one period" (p. 66). Britomart was her choice for an ideal woman not
only because she was virtuous but also because she was strong and
independent. Having mentioned Britomart several times, Fuller
eventually began to compare her with contemporary women. She
believed that Madame Roland was as valiant as Britomart and that
Mary Wollstonecraft and George Sand would not have become
outlaws had there been "as much room in the world for such, as in
Spenser's poem for Britomart" (p. 75). When a character like
Britomart satisfied her expectations, Fuller sounded as if she were
speaking of a real person and began to mix fictional with historical
women.

According to Fuller, having a woman monarch (whatever
Elizabeth's quality as a ruler) had its value in inspiring Spenser's
creation of epic women characters: "Unlike as was the English queen
to a fairy queen, we may yet conceive that it was the image of *a*
queen before the poet's mind that called up this splendid court of

women" (p. 66). If Queen Elizabeth helped to inspire Spenser, any strong woman inspired Fuller. She used her outstanding women—dead or alive, literary or historical or mythical—to witness the capabilities within women when they rely on themselves. Figures as disparate as Lady Godiva, Cinderella, George Sand, Mrs. Hutchinson, Cassandra, Eve, Hagar, and Venus served as testimonials in her sermons on the power within women.

This plethora of examples represents a remarkable amount of scholarship, and Fuller delved into countless sources in her search for answers. Although written in nineteenth-century language with some words as outmoded as *purity* and *delicacy* and a conversational style that might be considered affected, her work is surprisingly modern in its concepts. Her brilliant treatise presents and prefigures such modern ideas as the need for role models. Fuller searched beyond Judeo-Christian patriarchy for the feminine principle and the earth mother. She posited an androgenic quality in all people, a need to do away with sexual stereotyping. In essence, Fuller's creation becomes the archetype of woman, of "The Woman in the Nineteenth Century," and of any woman who has aspired, who has wondered and been thwarted but who has still refused to compromise. Fuller's archetypal woman knows that in any compromise, she compromises not only herself but everyone else as well; and that men who become exploiters suffer and lose their humanity themselves.

As with all scholarly and complex literature, reading *Woman* calls for active participation from readers. Also, since *Woman* is a highly suggestive work, readers must be receptive to its message. Both Edgar Allan Poe and Henry David Thoreau said that Fuller's writing and speaking voice were one. A careful scrutiny of *Woman* reveals the dynamism and insights that Fuller's conversation praised, and readers who are willing to become engaged in the profundity of her thought processes will be amply rewarded.

Essentially *Woman* is an affirmation, a witness to the possibilities within women and men who discover within themselves their spirituality and permit it to grow. It is a call for excellence. The first obstruction, the self, is on trial. Beginning with the individual, who must take responsibility for her or his own life, *Woman* envisions a world that would correspondingly reflect this changed self. Ultimately, *Woman* transcends the issue of woman's rights. Paradoxically, after preaching self-reliance for women, it becomes a philosophic message on the interdependence of all people.

*Woman in the Nineteenth Century*'s philosophic framework is predicated on universals; principles of right and wrong do indeed exist. Margaret Fuller was not ashamed to preach because she believed an individual could reshape her or his life—in fact, could approach perfection. And her sermon had effect. Early feminists were inspired to action by *Woman in the Nineteenth Century*. Three years after its publication, they called the first woman's rights convention in Seneca Falls, New York.


## NOTES

1. See Vivian C. Hopkins, "Margaret Fuller: Pioneer Women's Liberationist, *American Transcendental Quarterly* 18 (Spring 1973): 29–35. She writes: "Profusely illustrated and somewhat over-written, the book nevertheless has the effect of bringing the real closer to the ideal."

2. Thomas Wentworth Higginson, *Margaret Fuller Ossoli* (Boston: Houghton Mifflin, 1887), p. 200.

3. Another factor to consider in this discussion is that she wrote *Summer on the Lakes* between the publication of the earlier and later work. It served as a journey of self-discovery for Fuller, a means of crystallizing her thinking. Observing Indian and pioneer women in the West enlarged Fuller's perspective as to the hardships women had to endure.

4. F. O. Matthiessen, *American Renaissance* (London: Oxford University Press, 1941), pp. 24–31.

5. Julia Ward Howe, *Margaret Fuller (Marchesa Ossoli)* Boston: Little, Brown, 1905), p. 151; Arthur W. Brown, *Margaret Fuller* (New York: Twayne Publishers, 1964), p. 127.

6. In a letter (1841) that Alexander H. Everett wrote to Orestes A. Brownson, Everett referred to her as "Eurydice Fuller." George Willis Cooke, *An Historical and Biographical Introduction to Accompany the Dial* (1902; rpt., New York: Russell & Russell, 1961), 1: 79.

7. See Francis Edward Kearns, "Margaret Fuller's Social Criticism" (Ph.D. diss., University of North Carolina, 1960), p. 148: "As Edmund Berry has pointed out, 'some of the extracts from her reading look suspiciously like padding. . . . ' Moreover, one detects a faint aroma of pedantry about these long extracts. Frequently they appear to be totally out of

context and to be dragged in merely to illustrate Margaret's erudition. And not only is the style inflated, but it is annoyingly repetitious."

8.  Poe pointed out flaws in her style but concluded: "the style of Miss Fuller is one of the very best with which I am acquainted. In general effect, I know no style which surpasses it. It is singularly piquant, vivid, terse, bold, luminous; leaving details out of sight, it is everything that a style need be." *The Works of Edgar Allen Poe*, ed. Edmund Clarence Stedman and George Edward Woodberry (New York: Appleton-Crofts, 1951), 8:81.

# Chapter 6 Reception and influence

The impact of *Woman in the Nineteenth Century* was powerful. Serving as a catalyst, it generated the impulse to feminists to call the first woman's rights convention, which met in Seneca Falls. Still smarting from their snub at the 1840 World Anti-Slavery Convention in London, Elizabeth Cady Stanton and Lucretia Mott were inspired by *Woman* to organize this first convention in 1848.

Immediately after its publication in February 1845, *Woman in the Nineteenth Century* became a topic of controversy. Admirers applauded the courage of a woman who had voiced their unuttered thoughts. Detractors castigated her high ideals for marriage and her outspoken pleas for help and compassion for prostitutes. As Fuller wrote her brother in New Orleans, it was "the theme of all newspapers and many of the journals. Abuse public and private is lavished upon its views."[1] Selling at fifty cents a copy, sales of *Woman* were brisk, and many letters were exchanged in the wake of the excitement. Hawthorne's mother-in-law wrote to her daughter: "Margaret Fuller's book has made a breeze, I assure you."[2] On February 19, Charles Fenno Hoffman noted in a letter to Rufus Griswold: "Miss Fuller's 'Women [*sic*] in the Nineteenth Century' begins to make some talk."[3] At the time of publication, Mary A. Livermore wrote Fuller a note to express her "thankfulness." Many years later, in her lectures in behalf of woman's suffrage, she began with Fuller's

*Woman*, mentioning how far ahead of its time it was: "its appearance was the signal for an immediate widespread newspaper controversy, that raged with great violence."[4] Margaret Fuller herself was attacked for discussing sex since she was not married. Her sea captain suggestion became a source of laughter, but it also inspired supporters.

Many leading American and English newspapers and journals reviewed Fuller's work, and early reviews were, on the whole, favorable. The first review, in the February 8, 1845, *Boston Courier*, was written by Fuller's good friend, Lydia Maria Child. Four days later the review was reprinted in the paper for which Fuller wrote, the daily *New York Tribune*. After referring to Fuller as "a woman of more vigorous intellect and comprehensive thought than any other among the writers of this country," Child analyzed her style:

> It has the usual merits and defects of her style. It is strong, original, full of significance, abounding with learned allusions and eloquent expressions; but it is deficient in clearness, elaborate, and sometimes tangled in construction. The noble and beautiful thoughts of this author do not flow into orderly harmonious arrangements, or pause in musical cadences. To read her productions aloud is like walking through a grand forest, obstructed with underbush and stones, though rich in mosses and flowers. She always has too great profusion of materials. Her mind is like a room too much crowded with furniture. But a large and liberal mind it is, high in its aims, and pure in intentions.

Next she commended Fuller for her discussion of prostitution by using the euphemism "pollution," which she believed would cause her to be considered by many as "unpardonably bold." Child then confessed it was "a cheap effort" for her to praise a heroism that she would not have the "courage to practice."

The following day, February 13, 1845, the daily *New York Tribune* featured a second review of *Woman*, signed "C" (perhaps written by William Ellery Channing II). The author commended Fuller for her judgment and frankness and believed "the richness of illustration gives it value as a literary work. It should have a wide circulation among all classes, and awaken thought upon the great topics it treats with such ability." "C" was interested in reforming laws related to the property rights of women, but further than that, noted, "We are scarcely prepared to go. There is a fear lest delicacy and feminine loveliness will be sacrificed by all use in public of talent and accomplishment." On the whole, "C" wrote a favorable review, conceding that even thoughtful and generous men "have not a sufficient appreciation of Woman's nature to comprehend her wants, or to do justice to her claims."

Under the editorship of William Cullen Bryant, the *New York Evening Post* in a February 18, 1845, review recommended *Woman* to readers: "We should rejoice to know that it had been carefully read by every woman and man in this country." Although the reviewer found the style displeasing and the language "pretty strong and emphatic," he admired Fuller's vigor of thought, expression, and "remarkable freedom of spirit," as well as her demands for recognition of woman's dignity and spiritual rights.

By March, reviewers began not only to complain about her writing style but to attack Fuller herself. Her most vituperative critic was Charles F. Briggs, one of the editors of the *Broadway Journal*, who wrote three reviews in rapid succession during March. Briggs refuted her sea captains suggestion, declaring, "Woman cannot command." In his March 1 review, after deploring the length of the work, which he believed should be cut by two-thirds, and Fuller's choice of a title, Briggs introduced his strongest objection: "Woman is nothing but as a wife. How, then can she truly represent the female character who has never filled it? No woman can be a true woman, who has not been a wife and a mother." Then, attacking Fuller's disapproval of an isolated old wife who mindlessly lived in a barren spot for forty years because her husband wanted to do so, Briggs praised the woman "who had no thought but to please her husband." He ended his discussion of marriage with his choice of the perfect wife, Eloisa, who knew no law but her husband's will, "no happiness but his love." After Abelard was castrated ("dead to her through living"), Eliosa, Briggs exulted, was "true to him."[5]

In his "Second Notice" of March 8, 1845, Briggs complained that *Woman* "wants distinction," that it dealt with too much mythology—not enough with woman in the nineteenth century. After contending that "the difference between the sexes in this country is all in favor of the women," he added, "The privilege of voting is one which they could not exercise if it were granted." Again he reverted to his favorite argument: "The most direct writing is on a topic that no virtuous woman can treat justly, because she of necessity is imperfectly informed." Comparing capabilities of men and women, Briggs maintained: "As we have already said, the mind of woman is not endowed with the elements of command, because she cannot originate." This issue of the *Broadway Journal* also contained a "Portrait of a Distinguished Authoress," which, although not directly identified as Fuller, was easily recognized by all who had ever met her.[6] Above the engraving, a two-paragraph satiric sally included this description: "But for this, we would say, for example, that the nose is a little—a very little too Grecian—That the 'fine phrenzy' of the eyes has not been preserved so decidedly as it should be—that the chin has too shrewish a character—that the little finger of the left hand is too straight (or perhaps a little too crooked)—that the table is too round—the feather of the pen too feathery—and the ink (as far as we can judge of it through a metal ink-stand,) too *blue*." In a circular argument, Fuller thus was ridiculed for being an old maid and therefore presumably ignorant about sex; or if knowledgeable about sex, then as a woman who had lost her virtue. After attacking her ignorance or her lack of virtue, the *Broadway Journal* satirized her appearance. No wonder, then, that Fuller should write that it was not easy to lift her head "amidst the shower of public squibs and private sneers."[7]

Such personal attack, however, also brought Fuller some supporters. Defending his earlier reviews against their criticisms, Briggs claimed he was "strangely misrepresented." After reiterating his belief that an unmarried woman was not competent to talk about marriage, he reported that a meeting of young women was held in the superior court of the city hall to discuss ways that would enable them to earn their bread. To their plight he gave the pathetic suggestion that they take up the craft of wood engraving as a better means of making a living than by the needle. Perhaps the kindest thing that can be said about Briggs's rebuttal is that it attempted to address the problem of women's unemployment.

Not unlike Briggs in his preoccupation with sex, Orestes Augustus Brownson in his July 1845 issue of *Brownson's Quarterly Review* referred to Fuller's unconventional ideas: "Miss Fuller, in her *Woman in the Nineteenth Century* patronizes several renowned courtesans; and the chief ground of her complaint against our *masculine* social order seems to be, that it imposes undue restraints on woman's nature, and does not permit her to follow her natural sentiments and affections." Brownson also alluded to the practical *"jokes"* nature played (with the help of a young Adonis) on a poor girl "who was disgusted with conventionalism."[8]

Unlike Brownson and Briggs, however, Charles Lane sympathized with women and their sexual dilemmas. In a review in New Hampshire's *Herald of Freedom* (September 5, 1848), Lane acknowledged the sexual bondage of all women, especially of black women working in the fields and of white women working in factories, "for whom the royal palace and the peasant's cottage are alike scenes for the gratification" of man's "lowest lust." It follows then that it was a "monstrous absurdity" and "a cruel delusion" for men to believe they could be the instruments of a woman's elevation or her fair judge. No wonder his review, which evaluated *Woman* as "chaste and honorable, cheerful and faithful," was Fuller's favorite. Other favorable reviews appeared in *Graham's Magazine*, which said the work should be cherished, and in *Knickerbocker Magazine*, which described *Woman* as "well-reasoned and well-written." But Fuller's detractors persisted. In May 1845, the *Christian Examiner* found fault with Fuller's style; in April, *Ladies' National Magazine* argued that Fuller had attacked merely the social system, not its abuses, "where the real evil lies."

Another publication for women, *Godey's Magazine and Lady's Book*, featured the essay by Edgar Allan Poe that has become much quoted:

> "Woman in the Nineteenth Century" is a book which few women in the country could have written, and no woman in the country would have published, with the exception of Miss Fuller. In the way of independence, of unmitigated radicalism, it is one of the "Curiosities of American Literature," and Doctor Griswold should include it in his book. I need scarcely say that the essay is nervous, forcible, thoughtful, suggestive, brilliant, and to a certain extent scholarlike—for all that Miss Fuller produces is entitled to these

epithets—but I must say that the conclusions reached are
only in part my own. Not that they are too bold, by any
means—too novel, too startling, or too dangerous in their
consequences, but that in their attainment too many premises
have been distorted, and too many analogical inferences left
altogether out of sight. I mean to say that the intention of the
Deity as regards sexual differences—an intention which can
be distinctly comprehended only by throwing the exterior
(more sensitive) portions of the mental retina *casually* over the
wide field of universal analogy—I mean to say that this intention has not been sufficiently considered. Miss Fuller has
erred, too, through her own excessive subjectiveness. She
judges woman by the heart and intellect of Miss Fuller, but
there are not more than one or two dozen Miss Fullers on the
whole face of the earth.[9]

Poe echoed Briggs's review, which he disavowed—"She forgets
God created male and female"—when he assumed he was a better
interpreter of God's intentions than Fuller was. If Poe recognized
the difficulty in attaining Fuller's goals, he failed to perceive their
universality. Nevertheless, he did not fail to acknowledge her brilliance and uniqueness.

Not as well known as Poe's, but certainly as interesting, is a
review that appeared in the July 1846 issue of *Southern Quarterly
Review*. Although its attack on Fuller's ideas required more research
than those written to meet press deadlines, it represents thinking
current at the time, and the essay "The Condition of Women"
remains a classic sexist statement of stereotyped views about the
"weaker sex." Published in Charleston, South Carolina, the *Southern
Quarterly Review* featured a twenty-five-page review that discussed
woman from a historical and philosophical perspective. The essay
depicted the treatment of women in ancient Greece and Rome, in
early Germanic tribes, among American Indians and Australian
savages, and in contemporary China and India. The reviewer
pointed out the injustices in other societies—Indian squaws treated
as beasts of burden, the female infanticide widely practiced in
China—and, by way of contrast, considered American women for-
tunate to be treated so well and to have their own sphere of

influence. He argued that Christianity was responsible for the "elevation of woman." Contemporary woman had been "elevated in all things in which that equality was either practicable or desirable. She has been permitted, neither to command our armies nor to legislate in our senates, because for the one, she is incapacitated by her gentleness, and for the other, by her purity." "A.G.M." continued his polemic by refuting Fuller's ideas about love. Love was "but an episode with man," but love "forms the whole story of a woman's life." After speaking of woman's nervousness, her emotional nature, her passivity, and her coquetry, he argued that "the female organization" was characterized by "feebleness of muscle," making her dependent on men; hence, "her sense of dependence inspires her with a strong desire to please." If she sought intellectual distinction, she was "no longer a woman. She is unsexed, and though she may possess her power as a *litterateure*, she has none as a woman." Specifically referring to Fuller's sea captain passage, which he quoted along with several others, the author maintained: "This cannot be. . . . Woman may be worshipped as a deity, but it must not be as a Pallas." The author concluded, "In attempting to grasp the sceptre of an empire which her feeble strength can scarcely lift, woman loses the sovereignty of the heart where she has ever reigned with unrivalled sway."

Many women agreed with the assessment of the gentleman from South Carolina and were as hostile to *Woman* as were some of the male readers. Representative of a "lady's" point of view is Sophia Hawthorne's letter, written to her mother at the time of *Woman*'s publication. It is not surprising to learn that Sophia shared her husband's belief that a woman initiated into the mystery of sex would not be troubled by her rights. There is a trace of irony in her comment associating Fuller with royalty:

> What do you think of the speech which Queen Margaret Fuller has made from the throne? It seems to me that if she were married truly, she would no longer be puzzled about the rights of woman. This is the revelation of woman's true destiny and place, which can never be *imagined* by those who do not experience the relation. In perfect, high union there is no question of supremacy. Souls are equal in love and intelligent communion, and all things take their proper places as inevita-

bly as the stars their orbits. Had there never been false and profane marriages, there would not only be no commotion about woman's rights, but it would be Heaven here at once. Even before I was married, however, I could never feel the slightest interest in this movement. It then seemed to me that each woman could make her own sphere quietly, and also it was always a shock to me to have women mount the rostrum. Home, I think, is the great arena for women, and there, I am sure, she can wield a power which no king or conqueror can cope with. I do not believe any man who ever knew one noble woman would ever speak as if she were an inferior in any sense; it is the fault of ignoble women that there is any such opinion in the world.[10]

Sophia Hawthorne differed from other critics in that she blamed ignoble women for the inferior position of women in society. Mrs. Peabody, in their simultaneous exchange of letters, objected to Fuller's language as "offensive to delicacy." She believed that the book had the "look of absolute irreligion" and that genuine Christianity was the solution for everything. Although some reviewers did bring up the subject of Christianity and the story of Adam and Eve, most reviewers were tempered in their reaction to Fuller's statement that Christianity "has made no improvement" in woman's condition. The *London Quarterly Review* did mention the danger of her ideas and her lack of interest in Christianity in a review of the 1855 edition.

A letter pointing in the opposite direction, saying that Fuller was not pragmatic or radical enough, was written to her by John Neal, in acknowledgment of the copy of *Woman* she had sent him:

I have not been able to study your *Woman* as she deserves. And I have put off acknowledging her safe arrival (and delivery) day after day, in the hope of finding time to get well acquainted with her.

You go for thought—I, for action.

Women are fools—beyond all question. But who made them so? Their fathers—husbands—brothers—

I tell you that there is no hope for woman, til she has a hand in making the law—no chance for her til her *vote* is worth as

much as the man's vote. When it is—women will not be fobbed
off with six pence a day for the very work a man would get a
dollar for—[11]

No doubt Neal would have considered Sophia Hawthorne and her
mother the type of woman whom he dubbed a "fool." His crystal-
line analysis of the economic plight of women in 1845 anticipated the
realistic radicalism that was to dominate the feminist movement
after the Civil War.

With encouragement from John Neal and others, as well as newspaper reviews better than she might have had reason to expect,
Fuller was influenced to continue writing that developed the ideas
she had first postulated in *Woman*. The articles that poured forth
from her pen for the *New York Tribune* were written in New York and
later in Europe.

Some of her essays from the *New York Tribune*, as well as other
pieces, were collected by her brother, Arthur, and added as part II,
"Miscellanies," to his edition of *Woman*, which he first published in
1855 as *Woman in the Nineteenth Century, and Kindred Papers Relating to
the Sphere, Condition and Duties of Woman*. This edition has been
reprinted much more frequently than the first. In an introduction to
these widely disseminated essays, Horace Greeley declared they
were equally as worthy of consideration as was the original *Woman*.

As the subtitle indicates, the pieces the editor chose to reprint
were related to the problems confronting women. Loosely, the
"Miscellanies" could be divided into categories of education, man-
agement of a household, marriage, and old age. A recurrent thread
running throughout the works was that the societal ideal of a
woman's existence as a protected one was in opposition to the
reality, which was often a life of poverty. Although written in a
more straightforward, less exalted style than was *Woman*, these
essays expanded the themes previously begun there.

In her "Children's Books," Fuller offered some very good educational advice to parents. She did not think a forced moral should be
*de rigueur* in fiction, and she argued that children needed difficulties to be overcome. Their literature should tell the truth
instead of being "baby-house style," with stories of sex stereotyped
models of "sweet little girls and brave little boys" (p. 310). In

"Educate Men and Women as Souls," she postulated in succinct form material from her earlier work. Woman's power must be chartered so that she has every privilege a man has—"elective franchise, tenure of property, liberty to speak in public assemblies, etc." (p. 335). It is man's fault that an Aspasia or Ninon exists. Since society is complex and tasks that must be done are varied, it is no longer desirable to educate a girl merely for a domestic life. A large number of women are thrown on their own resources, and "sex, like rank, wealth, beauty, or talent, is but an accident of birth." Again apparently feeling it necessary to do so, she reassured men that "woman is born for love," but "men should deserve her love as an inheritance, rather than seize and guard it like a prey." Ultimately, man and woman, "as Apollo and Diana, twins of one heavenly birth" (p. 337), must not idealize each other but live for the glory of God.

With a similar theme concerning marriage, "Aglauron and Laurie" is a tale recounted in dialogue about a woman who made an unhappy first marriage at fifteen when she was too young to realize what marriage involved. When widowed and given a second chance to make a mature decision, she again married a man who did not live up to her expectations. In the conclusion of the story, Fuller wrote that as a consequence of her disappointment with her husband, the woman became too absorbed with her child. Instead she should live "as one link in a divine purpose" (p. 216). Thus as Fuller argued in *Woman*, she continued to assert that human earthly love had limitations; only by merging with the godhead could completeness be found.

Other articles concerned practical problems a wife had with housework and in dealing with servants. In "Household Nobleness" she found the besetting sin of housewives that of pettiness. Women were advised to keep their homes neat as a means to an end—the peace and joy of their families—rather than as an end in itself. In her discussion of ways of dealing with servants, most of whom at the time were Irish, she was again prescient. During a time when there was great hostility to the Irish immigrants in the United States, Fuller pointed out the great poetic faculties and natural eloquence of those who had to "begin the new life in the New World by doing all its drudgery" (p. 321). If employers were concerned about their servants' well-being, comfort, and feelings, then a people long oppressed would respond in kind.

As in her earlier work, Fuller continued her preoccupation in her subsequent essays with ideal women whom others could emulate. In "Glumdalclitches" and in her book review, "Ellen: or, Forgive and Forget," she again dealt with the possibilities of nobility in the female character. In "Woman's Influence over the Insane," she took an idealized stance as to the power of a gentle and kind woman in the treatment of the psychotic, and yet, her advocacy of more humane treatment of the mentally ill is in line with contemporary thinking on this subject.

Fuller's discussion of old age in the stages of a woman's lifetime is chilling because then, as now, many old women lived in poverty. In "Woman in Poverty" Fuller recounted the sad story of her old laundress, who did her backbreaking labor with dignity and looked forward to reunion with her family in heaven. "Ever Growing Lives" discussed the effect of old age on both men and women and concluded that not many old people have the developed character that the passage of time should bring.

In "The Wrongs of American Women: The Duty of American Women," Fuller discussed most cogently the issue of jobs for women. Her review of Charles Burdett's "The Wrongs of American Women" and of Catharine Beecher's "The Duty of American Women to Their Country," which was first printed in the *New York Tribune* on September 30, 1845, mentioned criticism of her *Woman in the Nineteenth Century*. Readers objected that she had exhibited the ills of society without "specifying any practical means for their remedy" (p. 226). Although she did not concede this point, she did delineate in greater detail than in her earlier work employment possibilities for women. She made it clear that women were never guaranteed financial support by a husband, brother, or father. Even were this true, a woman should still have other options. Since not all women could be assured of financial support, often they had "no choice but to work or steal, or belong to men, not as wives, but as the wretched slaves of sensuality" (p. 200). Therefore, more avenues of employment should be opened to them. She advocated that women be physicians or priests, but she did not believe there would be female lawyers. Then she recommended that more women be engaged as teachers and nurses. This review-essay has lost much of the transcendental tone of *Woman*. A realistic assessment of a woman's job prospects, it is a call for better-paying and more dignified employment opportunities for women.

When Margaret Fuller went to Europe, she continued to send dispatches to Horace Greeley that often had a focus on women and their problems. In England she described what could be considered a precursor of laundromats—washing and drying establishments. For poor people, there were public baths, as well as crèches, day-care centers for working mothers, she observed.

Fuller was well received in England because her book had already been pirated there during the year of its American publication. In an October 30, 1846, letter to Evert Augustus Duyckinck, an editor with the firm of Wiley and Putnam, she wrote: "I have been read here with a warmth that surprised me; it is chiefly to Woman in the Nineteenth Century that I am indebted for this; that little volume has been read and prized by many."[12] And when Fuller met Thomas and Jane Carlyle, she learned that Jane Carlyle, too, was pleased by *Woman*.

In Paris, she met and was charmed by the notorious George Sand. Her letters home reflected her fascination with Sand. Fuller was angered when she was turned away from a lecture at the Sorbonne. Her desire to hear Leverrier speak was thwarted when she was refused admission to the hall because of her sex, she wrote in a dispatch for the *New York Tribune*.

She continued to be concerned about the discrimination that women encountered in Italy. She described with sadness the cere-mony in which a woman took her vows as a nun, but she also mentioned with satisfaction that there was a woman Greek professor in Italy. Her dispatches, however, became centered on the de-teriorating political situation in Italy. She described the pope and the social unrest among the people as revolutionaries prepared for an abortive uprising, in which she and her lover participated.

Her reputation had proceeded her to Italy from England, so that she was able to meet Elizabeth Barrett and Robert Browning, with whom she became friends, and other members of the foreign intel-lectual circle and the local aristocracy. Despite the fact that the review of the influential British journal, the *Spectator*, criticized the style of her feminist treatise and said that *Woman* lacked profundity of thought, awareness of her work continued to grow among intellectual circles in Europe, as well as back in the United States.

The importance of Fuller's *Woman in the Nineteenth Century* is that it generated nationwide discussion of the problems women faced. The controversy aroused by issues Fuller gave utterance to in *Woman* continued to grow until it culminated in the first woman's rights convention, which was held in Seneca Falls, New York, July 19–20, 1848.[13] Lucretia Mott, Martha C. Wright, Mary Ann McClintock, and Elizabeth Cady Stanton issued the call to discuss the social, civil, and religious condition and rights of woman at Seneca Falls. At this convention, they wrote and adopted the Declaration of Sentiments. Although largely modeled after the Declaration of Independence, substituting *all men* for *King George*, the Declaration of Sentiments contains many of the ideas Fuller promulgated in *Woman*.[14] For example, Fuller's view of a woman's need for self-reliance was echoed: "He has endeavored, in every way that he could, to destroy her confidence in her own powers, to lessen her self-respect, and to make her willing to lead a dependent and abject life." Her belief that woman should live first for God appeared as: "He has usurped the prerogative of Jehovah himself, claiming it as his right to assign for her a sphere of action, when that belongs to her conscience and to her God." Fuller's refusal to accept the double standard of morality was used: "He has created a false public sentiment by giving to the world a different code of morals for men and women, by which moral delinquencies which exclude women from society, are not only tolerated, but deemed of little account in man." Other points that Fuller raised—such as a need for expanded employment opportunities—are mentioned. There is, however, a difference in tone between the Declaration of Sentiments and *Woman*. The Declaration of Sentiments largely lists grievances of women against men: "He has compelled her to submit to laws, in the formation of which she had no voice. He has withheld from her rights which are given to the most ignorant and degraded men—both natives and foreigners."[15] On the other hand, *Woman* reflects optimism. The Declaration of Sentiments ends with a realistic acknowledgment of the difficulties that awaited the feminist reformers and with a call for more conventions throughout the United States.

Although other local conventions were held, the first national women's rights convention was called for October 23–24, 1850, in Worcester, Massachusetts. In an account of this convention, the president, Paulina Wright Davis, wrote:

> One great disappointment fell upon us. Margaret Fuller, toward whom many eyes were turned as the future leader in this movement, was not with us. The "hungry ravening sea," had swallowed her up, and we were left to mourn her guiding hand—her royal presence. To her, I at least, had hoped to confide the leadership of this movement. It can never be known if she would have accepted it; the desire had been expressed to her by letter; but be that as it may, she was, and still is, a leader of thought; a position far more desirable than a leader of numbers.[16]

In addition to Davis's testimonial, given three months after Fuller's death, there is another one in the *History of Woman Suffrage* which goes into greater detail about contributions the leaders of the movement thought Fuller had made to their cause: "Margaret Fuller possessed more influence upon the thought of America, than any woman previous to her time. Men of diverse interests and habits of thought, alike recognized her power and acknowledged the quickening influences of her mind upon their own." Next the editors of the *History* lauded her as the "high-priestess" of the *Dial*, giving her precedence over Emerson and George Ripley. They continued enumerating her contributions:

> She sought to unveil the mysteries of life and enfranchise her own sex from the bondage of the past, and while still under thirty planned a series of conversations (in Boston) for women only, wherein she took a leading part. The general object of these conferences, as declared in her programme, was to supply answers to these questions: "What are we born to do?" and "How shall we do it?" or, as has been stated, "Her three special aims in those conversations were, To pass in review the departments of thought and knowledge, and endeavor to place

them in one relation to one another in our minds. To systematize thought and give a precision and clearness in which our sex are so deficient, chiefly, I think because they have so few inducements to test and classify what they receive. To ascertain what pursuits are best suited to us, in our time and state of society, and how we may make the best use of our means of building up the life of thought upon the life of action."

These conversations continued for several successive winters, and were in reality a vindication of woman's right to think. In calling forth the opinions of her sex upon Life, Literature, Mythology, Art, Culture, and Religion, Miss Fuller was the precursor of the Woman's Rights agitation of the last thirty-three years.[17]

Stanton had attended Fuller's conversations one winter in Boston[18] and started classes in Seneca Falls "in imitation of Margaret Fuller's Conversationals," which lasted for several years.[19] Next, the editors commended Fuller for writing "The Great Lawsuit; or, Man *vs.* Woman, Woman *vs.* Man" [*sic*], using Horace Greeley's evaluation as authoritative.

After quoting Fuller's idea that love is not a woman's whole existence, they continued their praise by discussing her accomplishments as a literary critic for the daily *New York Tribune* and how she had opened the way for other women to become journalists. The editors concluded their eulogy by emphasizing her femininity: "Theodore Parker, who knew her well, characterized her as a critic, rather than a creator or seer. But whether we look upon her as a critic, creator, or seer, she was thoroughly a woman. One of her friends wrote of her, 'She was the largest woman, and not a woman who wanted to be a man.' "[20]

The influence of Fuller's *Woman* continued to grow. In her reminiscences, Emily Collins, a leader of the Equal Suffrage Society in South Bristol, New York, wrote: "When I read the lectures of Ernestine L. Rose and the writings of Margaret Fuller, and found that other women entertained the same thoughts that had been seething in my own brain, and realized that I stood not alone, how my heart bounded with joy!"[21]

In addition to recognition given to Fuller by strangers, her influential friend, Horace Greeley, who had praised *Woman*, supported the feminist movement until after the Civil War. He attended conventions when he could, wrote letters of encouragement when he could not attend, and more importantly supported female emancipation in his daily *New York Tribune* at a time when many other newspapers, including the *New York Times*, the *New York Herald*, and the *Albany Register*, ridiculed the woman's suffrage movement. Although Greeley used to tease Fuller about her sea captain suggestion, he wrote to the officers of the Cleveland national convention three years after her death: "I recognize most thoroughly the right of woman to choose her own sphere of activity and usefulness, and to evoke its proper limitations. If she sees fit to navigate vessels, print newspapers, frame laws, select rulers—any or all of these—I know no principle that justifies man in interposing any impediment to her doing so."[22] Horace Greeley conceded at last what he had never done during Fuller's lifetime: if a woman wished to be a sea captain, she had the right to be one.

Greeley's letter by no means resolved the issue of women sea captains because Wendell Phillips brought the subject up again at the New England convention held in 1859:

Horace Greeley once said to Margaret Fuller: "If you should ask a woman to carry a ship round Cape Horn, how would she go to work to do it? Let her do this, and I will give up the question." In the fall of 1856, [*sic*] a Boston girl, only twenty years of age, accompanied her husband to California. A brain-fever laid him low. In the presence of mutiny and delirium, she took his vacant post, preserved order, and carried her cargo safe to its destined port. Looking in the face of Mr. Greeley, Miss Fuller said: "Lo! my dear Horace, it is done; now say, what shall women do next?" (Cheers).[23]

Although some mistake must have been made with the date of this incident, Fuller's sea captain suggestion seems to have caught the imagination of many people. Reference was made to this again in the *History* when the problem of jobs for women was discussed in more detail at the Tenth National Woman's Rights Convention held at the Cooper Institute, New York, May 10–11, 1860. Mrs. Elizabeth

Jones said: "I know that the conservative, in his fear, says, 'Surely you would not have woman till the soil, sail the seas, run up the rigging of a ship like a monkey (I use the language of one of our most distinguished men), go to war, engage in political brawls?' No! I would not have her do anything. She must be her own judge." After discussing other occupations for women, Jones returned to the navigation theme, again with humor:

> So far as navigation is concerned, I think many women would not be attracted to that life. There might be now and then a Betsy Miller, who could walk the quarter-deck in a gale, and that certainly would indicate constitutional ability to become a sailor. I do not suppose so much violence would be done to her nature by navigating the seas, as by helping a drunken husband to navigate the streets habitually. (Applause). In relation to running up the rigging like a monkey, or in regard to any other monkey performance, I do not believe that women will ever enter into competition with men in these things, because the latter have shown such remarkable aptitude for that business. (Laughter and applause).[24]

The point to be considered here is that the original impetus Fuller gave to the movement kept widening. As often happens with creative thinkers, they may be forgotten by those who have taken up their ideas and who reconstruct them in the vernacular of their own age.

In addition to Horace Greeley, other friends of Margaret Fuller prominent in the feminist movement included James Freeman Clarke, William Henry Channing, and Theodore Parker. Their knowledge of *Woman* helped to influence these transcendentalists to participate actively in the organized efforts of the suffragettes.

Another staunch supporter of the woman's rights cause was Thomas Wentworth Higginson, who knew Fuller when he was a child and later wrote her biography. In his speech on June 3, 1853, before the Committee of the Constitutional Convention of the Commonwealth of Massachusetts regarding qualifications of voters, he declaimed: "Believe me, it is easier to ridicule the petition of these women than to answer the arguments which sustain it." He concluded by using Ceres, one of Fuller's favorite illustrations from

mythology.[25] Devoting his life to liberal causes, Higginson published *Common Sense about Women* two years prior to his biography of
Fuller.[26] In *Common Sense*, he quoted Margaret Fuller as an authority
on the problems he discussed and used an allusion from *Woman*
when he referred to a group of western pioneers: "Those are the
future kings and queens."[27]

The importance of *Woman* as the major inspiration to the woman's
emancipation movement continued until well after the Civil War,
when it began a slow decline in influence. The publishing history of
*Woman* is a good index of its popularity. The original edition published by Greeley & McElrath was pirated in London for two
printings in 1845 and 1850. The next edition in the United States,
*Woman in the Nineteenth Century and Kindred Papers*, appeared in 1855,
with printings in Boston, Cleveland, and New York. A so-called
third edition was followed by one dated 1857 and then another in
1860, printed in Boston, New York, Philadelphia, and London.
This edition was printed again in 1862 during the Civil War. After
the war, editions appeared at least once in every decade of the
century: 1869, 1874, 1875, 1884, and 1893. No more editions of
*Woman* were published for seventy-five years.[28]

The era before the Civil War was a time of optimism among the
feminists, which matched the hopeful outlook of *Woman*. Women
met with some success with modification of property laws in state
legislatures, so they began to feel confident that after the Civil War
they would gain the ballot. Because many of the early proponents of
women's rights were also involved with the abolitionist movement,
they believed they would be given the vote along with the slaves
they had worked to free. The first great crisis in the movement came
after the war during debate over adoption of the Fourteenth
Amendment. Should the word *male* be appended to *inhabitant* for
the first time in the Constitution? In a bitter controversy the
feminists lost the support of Horace Greeley when he, along with
other men formerly sympathetic to the cause, said that now it was
the "Negro's Hour," and the time was not auspicious for the women
to press for the vote for themselves.[29] Even some of the former slaves
did not appear to be grateful for the help the women had given to
them and also failed to support their drive for the vote.[30] When the
women lost this battle in a lopsided vote, a new note of disillusion-

ment and increasing militancy appeared in their speeches and writing. Instead of calling their paper *Una* as formerly, their new publication was called the *Revolution*, symbolizing their changed mood.[31] Some women turned their interest to less idealistic writing, and after the Civil War, interest in *Woman* grew less intense.

The twentieth-anniversary woman's rights convention held in New York on October 19, 1870, expressed their mood of militancy.[32] Paulina Wright Davis in her resumé of the history of the woman's rights movement failed to mention Fuller although she praised Frances Wright at some length as a pioneer feminist and social activist who attempted to solve the problem of slavery.[33] As an example of a literary pioneer, Davis cited Sarah Helen Whitman as "the first literary woman of reputation who gave her name to the cause." However, she did mention the importance of *Woman* in a history of the movement she published the next year.[34] A new generation of feminists in a pragmatic push to win the ballot thought they could achieve better results from the collective pressure of organization than from the divine powers of intuition.

At no time, however, was *Woman* not influential during the nineteenth century. The people who had known Fuller continued to value her treatise, and as time passed, those who were attracted by the legend of her personality became acquainted with her work. Many of Fuller's ideas remained current and were reshaped by later feminists in more concrete, less romantic terms. Metaphors of growth and the need for self-reliance symbolized by the sea captain image still appeared in the speeches and writing of feminists. Occasional quotations from Goethe were used to embellish language that became more direct, less idealistic, and at times more ironic than horatory, Instead of admonishing, "Be ye perfect," feminists quoted statistics and argued fine points of law while interpreting the Constitution. However, the same issues Fuller had raised in *Woman* were still being discussed.

Margaret Fuller's influence extended into the twentieth century in the activities of four long-lived acquaintances: Caroline Healey Dall (1822–1912), Mary A. Livermore (1820–1905), Julia Ward Howe (1819–1910), and Ednah Dow Cheney (1824–1904). Dall, Howe, and Cheney had attended her conversations, and Livermore had met Fuller. All of these women lectured and wrote in behalf of the women's movement. In 1858, Dall emulated Fuller's conversations in her series of lectures given around the country under the general heading, "Woman's Claims to Education." Echoing *Woman*, Dall's lecture topics were: "Nov. 1st—The ideal standard of education, depressed by public opinion, but developed by the spirit of the age; Egypt and Algiers. Nov. 8th—Public opinion, as it is influenced by the study of the Classics and History, by general literature, newspapers, and customs. Nov. 15th—Public opinion, as modified by individual lives: Mary Wollstonecraft, Anna Jamieson [*sic*], Charlotte Bronte, and Margaret Fuller."[35] Mary A. Livermore's lecture, "What Shall We Do with Our Daughters?" was first delivered in 1867. She estimated that she gave this lecture eight hundred times in twenty-five years as she traveled throughout the country from Maine to Santa Barbara. Livermore's oft-repeated lecture began with a reference to *Woman in the Nineteenth Century*, which proclaimed truths and reforms, she later wrote, "far in advance of public acceptance." In her lecture, she interpreted Fuller's epigraphs in *Woman* to mean that "frailty" describes woman as she has been understood in the past, masqueraded in history and figured in literature. "The Earth waits for her Queen" prophesied the "grander type of woman, towards which to-day the whole sex is moving." Much of Livermore's lecture concerned practical advice about dress reform for women and health measures, employment, and education. But it ended on a religious, hopeful note, with "earthly life as the first school of the soul," characteristic of *Woman*.[36]

In a tacit admission that Fuller had been the subject of scandal—"pure as Una herself"—Cheney in her 1895 address before the Congress of American Advancement of Women, held in New Orleans, defended Fuller and her book:

Her wonderful book, "Woman in the Nineteenth Century," however easily criticised on the score of method, contains the pith and marrow of the woman movement, and makes the largest demand for her natural equality and political rights, and yet it brings her before you as pure as Una herself, claiming that it is by her fine spiritual power, by her sensitive conscience, by her open relation with the great spirit of life, that she is to become, "the Queen that the earth waits for."[37]

Shortly before her death, Cheney observed that there were Margaret Fuller clubs and Ossoli circles all over the country, and that on her last speaking tour, people in the "most unexpected places, in Dubuque," used to ask her about Fuller.[38]

Representing the thought of the new materialism, Julia Ward Howe in her biography of Fuller criticized *Woman* on scientific grounds: "Much is asserted about souls and their future which thinkers of the present day do not so confidently assume to know." At the same time, she noted that nothing written in later days had made "its teaching superfluous."[39] In her editing of the *Love-Letters of Margaret Fuller* (1903), she included an addendum containing excerpts from the *Memoirs* and from Charles Condon's *Reminiscences of a Journalist*. Echoing Emerson, Condon, who was acquainted with Fuller in Providence, wrote she was a "voluble talker" but "rather a careless writer," who "had a way of treating dissentients with a crisp contempt which was distinctly feminine."[40] Unwittingly, Howe was instrumental in helping to preserve the unattractive feminist portrait of the *Memoirs* and, in the edition of Fuller's love letters, giving people interested in scandal new grounds for speculation.

Another event that created renewed interest in Fuller was Julian Hawthorne's 1884 publication of his father's journal critical of Fuller. Referring to her book about "the never-to-be-exhausted theme of Woman's Rights," Julian reiterated his mother's view that married women were "not likely to be cordial supporters of such doctrines as the book enunciated."[41] This publication caused a number of articles to be written, both in Fuller's defense and by Julian supporting his father's attack. Its overall effect was to keep the scandal alive about Fuller's liaison with Ossoli. Hence her supporters emphasized her "purity" (as did Cheney) and defended her from the charge of arrogance in the *Memoirs* (which had a number of reprints). The women's movement found within their midst heroines as blameless as Susan B. Anthony who had voted to test the law.[42] Women applauded novelists who dramatized woman's plight: Charlotte Brontë, Elizabeth Gaskell, and George Eliot. After John Stuart Mill's "On the Subjection of Women" was published in 1867, they had a convincing case for female emancipation based on rational rather than spiritual arguments. Less credit needed to be given to *Woman* now that they had a well-organized treatise written by a man—the famous English author of "On Liberty"—to support their position.

Nevertheless, by the turn of the twentieth century, people were still aware of Fuller. A memorial pavilion was dedicated to her memory—"the John the Baptist of the women's movement"—at Point O'Woods, New York, in 1901. She was selected by a poll of readers of the *Christian Herald* in 1902 as one of twenty women to be in a Women's Hall of Fame.[43] Because the last publication of *Woman* was in 1893, copies of this work were becoming scarce. Mary Caroline Crawford wrote that *Woman* was remarkably prophetic and au courant with feminist thinking of 1910: "This article [*Woman*] might almost have been written for a suffragette organ in the year of our Lord, 1910, so extraordinarily fresh is it in tone and so nobly does it present the innate right of woman to real fulness of life." After explaining that *Woman* was almost inaccessible, she quoted passages for her readers.[44]

In addition to the unavailability of copies of *Woman*, other factors early in the twentieth century further tended to minimize the importance of *Woman*. The scientific theories that began in the nineteenth century were gaining more adherents, and as Julia Ward Howe had written, there was less confidence in the existence of souls. The Darwinian theory of evolution, biblical scholarship, and social scientists diminished the role of the individual, so crucial to Fuller's thesis.

Another social problem that increasingly won the attention of many feminists after the Civil War was alcoholism. Many people who had been associated with the abolitionist movement now transferred their reforming zeal to the drive for control of liquor that crystallized in the Temperance Union, bringing about prohibition before women's suffrage. Although Fuller briefly had mentioned the problem wives had with dissolute husbands and even intimated that they should be able to separate from them and have control over their children, she had not dwelt on this question or demanded passage of a law prohibiting the use of alcoholic beverages. Inspired by Carrie Nation's onslaught against the saloons and Alice Paul's imprisonment and hunger strikes, more women became active, participating in parades and picketing.

By the time of the ratification of the Nineteenth Amendment on

August 26, 1920, it is not surprising that there would have been an even greater loss of interest in *Woman*. Women had the ballot, and in the 1920s many people believed the battle for equal rights was over. In an investigation of early feminists, Augusta Genevieve Violette asserted five years after women had won the right to vote that "from the modern point of view the author of *Woman* had little of concrete value to propose in any way of a solution of the problem that she so intelligently stated."[45] In addition, the 1920s was an epoch during which Sigmund Freud became popular, so that the Fuller biographies that continued to appear concentrated on her search for love and her close attachment to her father rather than on her feminist work. The historian Mason Wade considered *Woman* to have been a "tract for the times" that caught on but that was little read when he published Fuller's biography in 1940.[46] Twenty-four years later, Arthur W. Brown concluded that *Woman* had been "almost entirely forgotten" in the twentieth century.[47]

After the depression and a series of wars during which most women seemed unconcerned with their rights in a society that largely had accepted the stereotype of the man-hating, frustrated feminist, a revival of interest in the problems confronting women reappeared. A concomitant need with the advent of the women's movement was for a retrospective look at the history of woman's struggle. Inevitably Fuller's *Woman* was rediscovered.[48] The historian Eleanor Flexner praised it as a "beacon to generations of women," and Betty Friedan cited Fuller's work in *The Feminine Mystique*.[49] The first printing in seventy-five years of *Woman in the Nineteenth Century, and Kindred Papers* was brought out in facsimile by Greenwood Press in 1968. Three more facsimile editions soon followed the eleventh printing, and a facsimile of the 1845 first edition will be printed in 1980 with an introduction by Madeleine Stern.

With new copies available, *Woman* became known to a wider audience. Popular *Ms.* magazine featured a Fuller biographical sketch and a few quotations from *Woman* in its "Lost Women" series in November 1972. The academic world, too, began to reflect this renewal of interest in the number of papers devoted to Fuller scholarship at recent annual meetings of the Modern Language Association of America.[50] Another response was the 1976 publication of *The*

*Woman and the Myth: Margaret Fuller's Life and Writings* by Bell Gale Chevigny. Although she acknowledged Fuller's role as a catalyst in the feminist movement, Chevigny's focus was on her political activism in Europe. The most recent biography, Paula Blanchard's *Margaret Fuller: From Transcendentalism to Revolution* (1978), again expressed the burgeoning interest in Fuller, and contained some analysis of concepts in *Woman*. Overall it delineated the difficulty a strong and brilliant woman encountered from society during the first half of the nineteenth century.

There seems little doubt that interest in *Woman in the Nineteenth Century*, and hence its influence, is increasing. *Woman* interests receptive feminists, of course, but also perceptive scholars concerned with the 1840s. Fuller's complex method of handling the disparate ideas of this period is unusual. Eighteenth-century rationalism and nineteenth-century socialism, transcendentalism, mythology, and world literature are synthesized from a unique feminist perspective.

*Woman* was both appropriate for its time and ahead of its time, as the feminist leaders themselves acknowledged soon after Fuller's death. Calling her the John the Baptist of the women's movement, they said she vindicated a woman's right to think. In 1845, *Woman in the Nineteenth Century* became the feminist manifesto, which was followed three years later by the women's declaration of independence, the Declaration of Sentiments. As the major inspiration of the feminist movement of the nineteenth century, Fuller engendered ideas that were catalytic to those who followed her. Many of her concepts are surprisingly modern. Due to the influence of Jung, much of the later twentieth-century literary criticism has been concerned with the use of myth. Fuller's *Woman*, which explored Scandinavian, classical, and biblical myths as a method of explaining the complexity of the human personality, is a precursor of mythic study. Psychologically intuitive, she understood the androgenous nature of sexuality and the conflict between women's need to love and their need for artistic expression, which often thwarted creative women. Her interest in Fourier is significant because of his psychological form of socialism, which considered an individual's emotional needs as important as his physical needs. *Woman* is of contemporary value as a starting point for feminist consciousness raising. Each woman is prompted to look within herself, at her past, and at her future goals. Ultimately it involves male consciousness raising, too, as a man is given to understand that he becomes psychically crippled when he enslaves others. In the process people are encouraged to look anew at works of literature and evaluate them for their honest presentation of female characters, as much as for their poetic skill.

Although some readers complained of the excessive interest in the soul of *Woman*, it should be clear that when Fuller did mention mundane reforms, she was uncompromising. Her most famous occupational suggestion—her sea captain image—caught the public imagination, and it still prevails as women fight for a chance to move from occupational ghettos. No doubt, as a young girl who lived near the coast of Massachusetts, in an age when Melville went off to sea, she had dreamed of the high adventure of going to sea. Unlike Melville, Fuller did not want to be an ordinary sailor; she wanted to command a ship. Her challenge that there could be a society that set no limits on a person because of sex is one that remains unfulfilled throughout the world.

Margaret Fuller realized that ultimately she represented the meaning of the transcendental age:

> The destiny of each human being is no doubt great and peculiar, however obscure its rudiments to our present sight, but there are also in every age a few in whose lot the meaning of that age is concentrated. I feel that I am one of those persons in my age and sex. I feel chosen among women. I have deep mystic feelings in myself and intimations from elsewhere.[51]

She incarnates the transcendental age. Her life and her work express American aspirations at their loftiest. Her *Woman* embodies the early American hope for a new Eden, the innocent ideal that, based on right principles, a just society is possible.

As a visionary, Margaret Fuller understood after writing *Woman in the Nineteenth Century* that the work was important and that it would endure: "Then I felt a delightful glow as if I had put a good deal of my true life in it, as if, suppose I went away now, the measure of my footprint would be left on the earth."[52] *Woman* is more than just a successful piece of protest propaganda that served its purpose as a means of arousing public opinion in its day. It has much to offer present and future generations of readers. Of all of the feminist writing, it is the most complex and the most spiritual. *Woman in the Nineteenth Century* most clearly delineates that it is in the interest of men as well as women that woman be able to fulfill herself: "That now the time has come when a clearer vision and better action are possible—when Man and Woman may regard one another as brother and sister, the pillars of one porch, the priests of one worship" (p. 172).

From the perspective of one living in the latter part of the twentieth century, it is at first surprising and then sobering to learn that the reception of *Woman in the Nineteenth Century* was as favorable as it was. It is disheartening to realize that initially less calumny was heaped on the ideas expressed in Fuller's treatise in 1845 than often has been hurled by both men and women at concepts expressed by feminists living today. Apparently people have not learned very much.

Is woman's liberation an idea whose time has come? As a concept, equality for women has been in origin and by analogy intrinsically linked with chattel slavery. Before the Civil War, many women were less timid about demanding abolition of slavery than they were in demanding their own emancipation. So, too, is it today. When the great idea that racial and ethnic prejudice is unethical is taking hold within the intellectual establishment and society at large, the idea that sexual prejudice is equally destructive is much slower to win acceptance.

When the time comes, if it ever comes, that women can develop their talents and their souls without undue impediment, there will be an explosion of genius and insight, the dimensions of which the world has not yet seen. At present, though, the earth still waits for the coming of the Queen that Margaret Fuller invoked so long ago.

*NOTES*

1. Letter from Margaret to Eugene, February 1845, in *The Writings of Margaret Fuller*, ed. Mason Wade (New York: Viking Press, 1941), p. 575.

2. Julian Hawthorne, *Nathaniel Hawthorne and His Wife* (Boston: Houghton Mifflin, 1884), I: 257.

3. Homer F. Barnes, *Charles Fenno Hoffman* (New York: Columbia University Press, 1930), p. 256.

4. Mary A. Livermore, *The Story of My Life* (Hartford: A. D. Worthington & Co., 1898), pp. 592, 615.

5. Of this review Poe wrote, "I still feel myself called upon to disavow the silly, condemnatory criticism of the work which appeared in one of the earlier numbers of the 'Broadway Journal.' That article was *not* written by myself, and *was* written by my associate, Mr. [Charles F.] Briggs." C. F. Briggs, Poe, and H. C. Watson were editors at the time. Edgar Allan Poe, *The Complete Works of Edgar Allan Poe*, ed. Edmund Clarence Stedman and George Edward Woodberry (New York: The Colonial Company, 1895), 8:77.

6. Joel Myerson identifies this engraving as Fuller in *Margaret Fuller: An Annotated Secondary Bibliography* (New York: Burt Franklin, 1977), p. 10.

7. James Russell Lowell dedicated his satiric volume of poetry containing "A Fable for Critics," published in 1848: "To Charles F. Briggs, This Volume Is Affectionately Inscribed."

8. *The Works of Orestes A. Brownson*, ed. Henry F. Brownson (1845; rpt., New York: AMS Press, 1966), 6:39.

9. Poe, *Complete Works*, 8:76–77.

10. *Nathaniel Hawthorne and His Wife*, 1:257.

11. Letter from John Neal, February 28, 1845, Fuller MSS, 11:117, Houghton Library, Harvard University. Reprinted by permission of the Houghton Library.

12. "Margaret Fuller on Literary London in 1846," *New York Public Library Bulletin* 5 (1901): 455. Originally this article was a letter written by Fuller and subsequently reproduced by the *Bulletin*.

13. The first volume of the history of the woman's suffrage movement was published in 1881. The editors were all leaders of the agitation for women's rights during the last century; therefore, their volumes are major source material for scholars. Elizabeth Cady Stanton, Susan B. Anthony, and Matilda Joslyn Gage, eds., *History of Woman Suffrage* (New York: Fowler & Wells, 1881–87).

14. The editors called it a "parody of the Fathers of '76." Ibid., 1:129.

15. Ibid., pp. 70–71.

16. Ibid., p. 217.

17. Ibid., pp. 801–802.

18. Faith Chipperfield, *In Quest of Love* (New York: Coward-McCann, 1957), p. 300.

19. Elizabeth Cady Stanton, *Eighty Years and More* (New York: Harper, 1898), p. 152.

20. Stanton, Anthony, and Gage, *History*, 1:802.

21. Ibid., p. 89.

22. Ibid., p. 125.

23. Ibid., p. 276.

24. Ibid., pp. 697–698.

25. Ibid., p. 252. Higginson presided at the unusual wedding ceremony of Henry B. Blackwell and Lucy Stone in West Brookfield in 1855. A written protest against the Blackstone code, which made woman a nonentity in marriage, was appended to the marriage ceremony, in which the bride refused to take her husband's name. Higginson wrote a preface to the protest: "I never perform the marriage ceremony without a renewed sense of the iniquity of our present system of laws in respect to marriage: a system by which 'man and wife are one, and that one is the husband.' It was with my hearty concurrence, therefore, that the following protest was read and signed, as a part of the nuptial ceremony; and I send it to you, that others may be induced to do likewise." Ibid., p. 260.

26. Higginson commanded the first American regular army regiment of freed slaves during the Civil War. There has been a revival of interest in Higginson's account of his experiences in *Army Life in a Black Regiment*, with a new introduction by Howard N. Meyer (New York: Collier Books, 1969).

27. Thomas Wentworth Higginson, *Common Sense about Women* (Boston: Lee and Shepard Publishers, 1882), p. 327.

28. Joel Myerson, *Margaret Fuller: A Descriptive Primary Bibliography* (Pittsburgh: University of Pittsburgh Press), 1978.

29. See Stanton, Anthony, and Gage, *History*, 2:101, which records a *New York Tribune* editorial: "The sure panacea for such ills as the Massachusetts petitioners complain of, is a wicker-work cradle and a dimple-cheeked baby." This echoes Greeley's comment about Fuller: "Noble and great as she was, a good husband and two or three bouncing babies would have emancipated her from a good deal of cant and nonsense." Horace Greeley, *Recollections of a Busy Life* (New York: J. B. Ford & Co., 1869), p. 178.

30. Stanton, Anthony, and Gage, *History*, 2:90–91, 314–344.

31. Ibid., p. 319.

32. A celebration of Fuller's sixtieth birthday was held in 1870 at the Woman's Club. Writing that Clarke, Hedge, Channing, Cranch, Mr. and Mrs. Spring, Miss Peabody, Mrs. Cheney, Higginson, and Mrs. Howe all "bear eloquent testimony to her exalted character and genius," Alcott repeated in his journal what most people had come to believe, that Fuller

was a better conservationalist than writer. *The Journals of Bronson Alcott*, ed. Odell Shepard (Boston: Little, Brown, 1938), p. 409.

33. Stanton, Anthony, and Gage, *History*, 2:429.

34. Ibid., p. 433.

35. Ibid., 1:262.

36. Mary A. Livermore, *The Story of My Life* (Hartford, Conn.: A. D. Worthington & Co., 1898), pp. 492, 615–629.

37. Ednah Dow Cheney, *Reminiscences of Ednah Dow Cheney* (Boston: Lee and Shepard, 1902), p. 194.

38. Mary Caroline Crawford, *Romantic Days in Old Boston* (Boston: Little, Brown, 1910), p. 73.

39. Julia Ward Howe, *Margaret Fuller (Marquesa Ossoli)* (Boston: Little, Brown, 1905), pp. 152–153.

40. Margaret Fuller, *Love-Letters of Margaret Fuller, 1845–1846*, ed. Julia Ward Howe (1903; rpt., New York: Greenwood Press, 1969), pp. 224–228.

41. *Nathaniel Hawthorne and His Wife*, 1:256.

42. See Stanton, Anthony, and Gage, *History*, 2:647–701. Anthony was convicted in Canandaigua, New York, after her trial on June 17–18, 1873.

43. Myerson, *Secondary Bibliography*, pp. 105–106.

44. Mary Caroline Crawford, *Romantic Days in Old Boston* (Boston: Little, Brown, 1910), pp. 61, 74–75. Little known today, Crawford (1874–1932) also wrote *In the Days of the Pilgrim Fathers*, *Old Boston Ways*, and *Among Old New England Inns*.

45. Augusta Genevieve Violette, *Economic Feminism in American Literature Prior to 1848* (Orono, Maine: University Press, 1925), p. 87.

46. Mason Wade, *Margaret Fuller: Whetstone of Genius* (New York: Viking Press, 1940), pp. 134–135.

47. Arthur W. Brown, *Margaret Fuller* (New York: Twayne Publishers, 1964), pp. 127–133.

48. For a survey of the last thirty years of research, see Madeleine Stern's "A Biographer's View of Margaret Fuller," *AB Bookman's Weekly* 53 (February 4, 1974): 427–428.

49. Eleanor Flexner, *Century of Struggle: The Woman's Rights Movement in the United States* (Cambridge, Mass.: Belknap Press, 1959), p. 66.

50. See Margaret V. Allen's "This Impassioned Yankee: Margaret Fuller's Writing Revisited," *Southwest Review* (Spring 1973): 162–171.

51. *Love-Letters of Margaret Fuller*, pp. 21–22.

52. *The Writings of Margaret Fuller*, ed. Mason Wade (New York: Viking Press, 1941), p. 567.

# Selected bibliography

Abel, Darrell. "Hawthorne on the Strong Division-Lines of Nature." *American Transcendental Quarterly* (Spring 1972): 23–31.

Alcott, A. Bronson. *The Journals of Bronson Alcott.* Edited by Odell Shepard. Boston: Little, Brown, 1938.

_____. *The Letters of A. Bronson Alcott.* Edited by Richard L. Herrnstadt. Ames, Iowa: Iowa State University Press, 1969.

Allen, Margaret V. "This Impassioned Yankee: Margaret Fuller's Writing Revisited." *Southwest Review* (Spring 1973): 162–171.

Anthony, Katharine. *Margaret Fuller, a Psychological Biography.* New York: Harcourt, Brace and Howe, 1920.

Baer, Helene G. "Mrs. Child and Miss Fuller." *New England Quarterly* 26 (June 1953): 249–255.

_____. *The Heart Is Like Heaven: The Life of Lydia Maria Child.* Philadelphia: University of Pennsylvania Press, 1964.

Beach, Seth Curtis. *Daughters of the Puritans.* Boston: American Unitarian Association, 1907.

Bell, Margaret. *Margaret Fuller.* New York: Charles Boni, 1930.

Blanchard, Paula. *Margaret Fuller: From Transcendentalism to Revolution.* New York: Delacorte Press, 1978.

Braun, Frederick Augustus. *Margaret Fuller and Goethe.* New York: Henry Holt, 1910.

Brooks, Gladys. *Three Wise Virgins.* New York: E. P. Dutton, 1957.

Brooks, Van Wyck. *The Flowering of New England, 1815–1865.* 52d ed. New York: E. P. Dutton, 1940.

Brown, Arthur W. *Margaret Fuller*. Twayne's "United States Authors" Series. New York: Twayne Publishers, 1964.

Brown, Charles Brockden. *Alcuin: A Dialogue*. 1798. Rpt., New Haven: Carl and Margaret Rollins, 1935.

———. *Ormond*. Edited by Ernest Marchand. New York: Hafner, 1962.

———. *Wieland; or, The Transformation*. Port Washington, N.Y.: Kennikat Press, 1963.

Brownson, Orestes A. *The Works of Orestes A. Brownson*. Edited by Henry F. Brownson. New York: AMS Press, 1966.

Burton, Roland Crozier. "Margaret Fuller's Criticism: Theory and Practice." Ph.D. dissertation, State University of Iowa, 1941.

Cheney, Ednah Dow. *Reminiscences of Ednah Dow Cheney*. Boston: Leo and Shepard, 1902.

Chevigny, Bell Gale. *The Woman and the Myth: Margaret Fuller's Life and Writings*. Old Westbury, N.Y.: Feminist Press, 1976.

Child, Mrs. [Lydia]. *An Appeal in Favor of That Class of Americans Called Africans*. Boston: Allen and Ticknor, 1833.

———. *The History of the Condition of Women in Various Ages and Nations*. 2 vols. Boston: Otis, Broaders & Co., 1838.

———. *Madame de Stael. Madame Roland*. N.p., [1832].

———. *The Mother's Book*. Boston: Carter and Hendes, 1831.

———, ed. *The Oasis*. Boston: Allen and Ticknor, 1834.

Chipperfield, Faith. *In Quest of Love*. New York: Coward-McCann, 1957.

Colville, Derek. "The Transcendental Friends: Clarke and Margaret Fuller." *New England Quarterly* 30 (September 1957): 378–382.

Cooke, George Willis. *An Historical and Biographical Introduction to Accompany The Dial*. 1902. Rpt., New York: Russell & Russell, 1961.

Crawford, Mary Caroline. *Romantic Days in Old Boston*. Boston: Little, Brown, 1910.

Culligan, Glendy. "Review of Joseph Jay Deiss's *The Roman Years of Margaret Fuller*." *Saturday Review*, December 20, 1969, pp. 27, 73.

Deiss, Joseph Jay. "Humanity, Said Edgar Allan Poe, Is Divided into Men, Women, and Margaret Fuller." *American Heritage* 23 (August 1972): 43–47, 94–97.

———. *The Roman Years of Margaret Fuller*. New York: Thomas Y. Crowell, 1969.

Eliot, George. "Margaret Fuller and Mary Wollstonecraft." *The Leader*. 1855. Rpt., *The Norton Anthology of English Literature*. Edited by M. H. Abrams et al. 3d ed. New York: W. W. Norton, 1974. 2:1322–1328.

Emerson, Ralph Waldo. *Essays by Ralph Waldo Emerson*. Boston: Houghton Mifflin, 1883.

_____. *The Collected Works of Ralph Waldo Emerson*. Edited by Robert E. Spiller. Cambridge: Harvard University Press, 1971.

_____. *The Correspondence of Emerson and Carlyle*. Edited by Joseph Slater. New York: Columbia University Press, 1964.

_____. *The Early Lectures of Ralph Waldo Emerson*. Edited by Stephen E. Whicher, Robert E. Spiller, and Wallace E. Williams. Cambridge: Harvard University Press, 1964.

_____. *The Journals and Miscellaneous Notebooks of Ralph Waldo Emerson*. Edited by William H. Gilman et al. Cambridge: Harvard University Press, 1960.

_____. *Journals of Ralph Waldo Emerson*. Edited by Edward Waldo Emerson and Waldo Emerson Forbes. Boston: Houghton Mifflin, 1911–1912.

_____. *The Letters of Ralph Waldo Emerson*. Edited by Ralph L. Rusk. 6 vols. New York: Columbia University Press, 1939.

_____, et al. *Memoirs of Margaret Fuller Ossoli*. 2 vols. Boston: Phillips, Sampson, 1852.

Fay, Josephine J. [Sister Francis Michael, S.C.H.]. "Margaret Fuller, Literary Critic." Ph.D. dissertation, St. John's University, Brooklyn, 1951.

Flexner, Eleanor. *Century of Struggle: The Woman's Rights Movement in the United States*. Cambridge: Belknap Press of Harvard University Press, 1959.

Fourier, François Marie Charles. *Oeuvres complètes de Ch. Fourier*. Paris: Librairie Societaire, 1841–1848.

_____. *The Utopian Vision of Charles Fourier:* Selected, translated, edited, and with an introduction by Jonathan Beecher and Richard Bienvenu. Boston: Beacon Press, 1971.

Friedan, Betty. *The Feminine Mystique*. 6th ed. New York: Dell Publishing, 1964.

Frothingham, Octavius Brooks. *Transcendentalism in New England: A History*. Edited by Sydney E. Ahlstrom. 1876. Rpt., Gloucester, Mass.: Peter Smith, 1965.

Fuller, Margaret. [Sarah Margaret Fuller Ossoli]. *Art, Literature and the Drama*. Edited by A. B. Fuller. 1860. Rpt., Boston: Roberts Bros., 1889.

_____. *At Home and Abroad, or Things and Thoughts in America and Europe*. Edited by Arthur B. Fuller. 1856. Rpt., Port Washington, N.Y.: Kennikat Press, 1971.

_____. *Conversations with Goethe, from the German of Eckermann*. Trans. Boston: Hilliard, Gray, 1839.

_____. *The Dial: A Magazine for Literature, Philosophy, and Religion*. 4 vols. 1840–1844. Rpt., New York: Russell & Russell, 1961.

————. *Life Without and Life Within*. Edited by A. B. Fuller. Boston: Brown, Taggard and Chase, 1859.

————. *Literature and Art*. Introduction by Horace Greeley. New York: Fowlers and Wells, 1852.

————. *Love-Letters of Margaret Fuller, 1845–1846*. Introduction by Julia Ward Howe. 1903. Rpt., Westport, Conn.: Greenwood Press, 1969.

————. *Margaret Fuller: American Romantic: A Selection from her Writings and Correspondence*. Edited by Perry Miller. 1963. Rpt., Ithaca, N.Y.: Cornell University Press, 1970.

————. "Margaret Fuller on Literary London." [Letter from Margaret Fuller to Duyckinck, London, October 30, 1846.] *New York Public Library Bulletin* 5 (1901): 455–456.

————. *Woman in the Nineteenth Century and Kindred Papers Relating to the Sphere, Condition and Duties of Women*. Edited by Arthur B. Fuller with introduction by Horace Greeley. Boston: John P. Jewitt, 1855.

————. *The Writings of Margaret Fuller*. Edited by Mason Wade. New York: Viking Press, 1941.

Fuller Papers and Manuscripts. Boston Public Library.

————. Harvard University. Houghton Library. Vols. 1–17.

Fuller, Richard Frederick. "The Younger Generation in 1840 from the Diary of a New England Boy." *Atlantic Monthly* 136 (August 1925): 216–224.

Goddard, Harold Clarke. "Transcendentalism." *The Cambridge History of American Literature*. Edited by William Peterfield Trent et al. New York: Putnam's, 1917.

Goethe, Johann Wolfgang von. *Faust*. Translated by Bayard Taylor. New York: Modern Library, 1930.

————. *The Sufferings of Young Werther*. Translated by Harry Steinhauer. New York: W. W. Norton, 1970.

————. *Wilhelm Meister's Apprenticeship*. Translated by Thomas Carlyle. New York: Heritage Press, 1959.

Greeley, Horace. *Recollections of a Busy Life*. New York: J. B. Ford, 1868.

Hale, Sarah Josepha. *Woman's Record*. 1855. Rpt., New York: Source Book Press, 1970.

Harper, Ida Husted. *The Life and Works of Susan B. Anthony*. Indianapolis: Hollenbeck Press, 1898.

Hawthorne, Julian. *Nathaniel Hawthorne and His Wife*. 2 vols. Boston: Houghton Mifflin, 1884.

Hawthorne, Nathaniel. *The Blithedale Romance*. Introduction by Arlin Turner. New York: W. W. Norton, 1958.

————. *The Marble Faun*. Edited by Richard H. Rupp. Indianapolis: Bobbs-Merrill, 1971.

————. *The Scarlet Letter*. London: Thomas Nelson and Sons, n.d.

Healey, Caroline W. [Dall]. *Margaret and Her Friends*. Boston: Roberts Brothers, 1895.

Higginson, Thomas Wentworth. *Common Sense about Women*. Boston: Lee and Shepard, 1882.

———. *Margaret Fuller Ossoli*. Boston: Houghton Mifflin, 1887.

Holmes, Oliver Wendell. "Cinders from Ashes." *Atlantic Monthly* 23 (January 1869): 115–123.

———. *Elsie Venner—A Romance of Destiny*. Boston: Houghton Mifflin, 1887.

———. *A Mortal Antipathy*. Boston: Houghton Mifflin, 1885.

Hopkins, Vivian C. "Margaret Fuller: Pioneer Women's Liberationist." *American Transcendental Quarterly* 18 (Spring 1973): 29–35.

Howe, Julia Ward. *Margaret Fuller (Marchesa Ossoli)*. Boston: Little, Brown, 1905.

James, Henry. *The Bostonians*. 1886. Rpt., New York: Dial Press, 1945.

———. *William Wetmore Story and His Friends*. 1903. Rpt., New York: Grove Press, 1957.

Jameson, Mrs. [Anna]. *Memoirs of Celebrated Female Sovereigns*. 2d ed. London: George Toutledge and Sons, n.d.

———. *Memoirs of the Loves of the Poets*. Boston: Houghton Mifflin, 1900.

———. *Shakespeare's Heroines*. London: George Ball & Sons, 1897.

———. *Visits and Sketches at Home and Abroad, with Tales and Miscellanies now first collected, and a new edition of the "Diary of an Ennuyée."* 2 vols. New York: Harper and Brothers, 1834.

———. *Winter Studies and Summer Rambles in Canada*. 3 vols. London: Saunders and Otley, 1838.

Jones, Louis C. "A Margaret Fuller Letter to Elizabeth Barrett Browning." *American Literature* 9 (March 1937): 70–71.

Kearns, Francis Edward. "Margaret Fuller's Social Criticism." Ph.D. dissertation, University of North Carolina, 1961.

Kirdl, Manfred, ed. *Adam Mickiewicz: Poet of Poland, A Symposium*. New York: Columbia University Press, 1951.

Landor, Walter Savage. *The Longer Prose Works of Walter Savage Landor*. Edited by Charles G. Crump. 2 vols. London: J. M. Dent, 1893.

McMaster, Helen Neill. "Margaret Fuller as a Literary Critic." *University of Buffalo Studies* 7 (December 1928): 31–100.

Martineau, Harriet. *Retrospect of Western Travel*. 2 vols. London: Saunders and Otley, 1838.

———. *Society in America*. 2 vols. 4th ed. New York: Saunders and Otley, 1837.

Matthiessen, F. O. *American Renaissance*. London: Oxford University Press, 1941.

Maurois, André. *Leila: The Life of George Sand*. Translated by Gerard Hopkins. London: Jonathan Cape, 1953.

Maynard, Theodore. *Orestes Brownson: Yankee, Radical, Catholic*. New York: Macmillan, 1943.

180                                                Selected Bibliography

Meyer, Howard N. *Colonel of the Black Regiment: The Life of Thomas Wentworth Higginson.* New York: W. W. Norton, 1967.

Mill, John Stuart. *Three Essays On Liberty, Representative Government, The Subjection of Women.* Introduction by Millicent Garrett Fawcett. London: Oxford University Press, 1912.

Miller, Perry. " 'I Find No Intellect Comparable to My Own.' " *American Heritage* 8 (February 1957): 22–25, 96–99.

――――, ed. *The American Transcendentalists.* Garden City, N.Y.: Doubleday, 1957.

――――, ed. *Margaret Fuller: American Romantic.* 1936. Rpt., Ithaca, N.Y.: Cornell University Press, 1970.

――――. *The Transcendentalists, An Anthology.* Cambridge: Harvard University Press, 1950.

Myerson, Joel. "An Annotated List of Contributions to the Boston *Dial.*" *Studies in Bibliography* 26 (1973): 133–166.

――――. "Bronson Alcott's 'Scripture for 1840.' " *ESQ: A Journal of the American Renaissance* 20 (Fourth quarter 1974): 236–259.

――――. "A Calendar of Transcendental Club Meetings." *American Literature* 44 (May 1972): 197–207.

――――. "Caroline Dall's Reminiscences of Margaret Fuller." *Harvard Library Bulletin* 22 (October 1974): 414–428.

――――. "Frederic Henry Hedge and the Failure of Transcendentalism." *Harvard Library Bulletin* 23 (October 1975): 369–410.

――――. *Margaret Fuller: A Descriptive Bibliography.* Pittsburgh: University of Pittsburgh Press, 1978.

――――. *Margaret Fuller: An Annotated Secondary Bibliography.* New York: Burt Franklin, 1977.

――――. "Margaret Fuller's 1842 Journal: At Concord with the Emersons." *Harvard Library Bulletin* 21 (July 1973): 320–340.

――――. " 'In the Transcendental Emporium': Bronson Alcott's 'Orphic Sayings' in the *Dial.*" *English Language Notes* 10 (September 1972): 31–38.

――――. " 'A True & High Minded Person': Transcendentalist Sarah Clarke." *Southwest Review* 59 (Spring 1974): 163–172.

Oberndorf, Clarence P. *The Psychiatric Novels of Oliver Wendell Holmes.* New York: Columbia University Press, 1943.

Owen, Robert Dale. *Popular Tracts,* No. 1. New York: Office of the Free Enquirer, 1830.

Parrington, Vernon L. *Main Currents in American Thought.* Vol. 2: *The Romantic Revolution in America.* New York: Harcourt, Brace, 1930.

Payne, William Morton, ed. *American Literary Criticism.* 1904. Rpt., Freeport, New York: Books for Libraries Press, 1968.

Poe, Edgar Allan. *The Works of Edgar Allan Poe.* Edited by Edmund Clarence
    Stedman and George Edward Woodberry. Vol. 8. New York: The
    Colonial Company, 1895.
Quinn, Arthur Hobson. "The Establishment of National Literature." In *The
    Literature of the American People.* Edited by Arthur Quinn, pp. 175–566.
    New York: Appleton-Crofts, 1951.
Ringe, Donald A. *Charles Brockden Brown.* Twayne's "United States Authors"
    Series. New York: Twayne Publishers, 1966.
Rosenthal, Bernard. "*The Dial*, Transcendentalism and Margaret Fuller." *English
    Language Notes* 8 (September 1970): 28–36.
Ross, Donald. "Dreams and Sexual Repression in *The Blithedale Romance.*" *PMLA*
    86 (October 1971): 1014–1017.
Rostenberg, Leona. "The Diary of Timothy Fuller in Congress, January
    12–March 15, 1818." *New England Quarterly* 12 (September 1939):
    521–529.
Rowson, Susanna. *Charlotte Temple: A Tale of Truth.* Edited by Clara M. and
    Rudolf Kirk. 1791. Rpt., New Haven: College & University Press, 1964.
Rusk, Ralph L. *The Life of Ralph Waldo Emerson.* New York: Scribner's, 1949.
Sams, Henry W., ed. *Autobiography of Brook Farm.* Englewood Cliffs, N.J.:
    Prentice-Hall, 1958.
Sand, George. *Mauprat.* Boston: Roberts Brothers, 1893.
Schlesinger, Arthur M., Jr. *Orestes A. Brownson: A Pilgrim's Progress.* Boston:
    Little, Brown, 1939.
Sedgwick, Catharine Maria. *Live and Let Live: or Domestic Service Illustrated.* New
    York: Harper & Brothers, 1837.
———. *Means and Ends, or Self-training.* 2d ed. New York: Saunders and Otley,
    1837.
Shapiro, Fred C. "The Transcending Margaret Fuller." *Ms.* 2 (November 1972).
Shepard, Odell. *Pedlar's Progress: The Life of Bronson Alcott.* Boston: Little, Brown,
    1937.
Staël, Madame de. *Corinne: or Italy.* Translated by Emily Baldwin and Pauline
    Driver. London: George Bell & Sons, 1890.
Stanton, Elizabeth Cady, et al. *History of Woman Suffrage.* 2 Vols. New York:
    Fowler & Wells, 1881.
Stern, Madeleine. "A Biographer's View of Margaret Fuller." *AB Bookman's
    Weekly* 53 (February 4, 1974): 427–428.
———. *The Life of Margaret Fuller.* New York: E. P. Dutton, 1942.
Strauch, Carl F. "Hatred's Swift Repulsions: Emerson, Margaret Fuller, and
    Others." *Studies in Romanticism* 7 (Winter 1968): 65–103.
Thomas, Clara. *Love and Work Enough: The Life of Anna Jameson.* Toronto: Univer-
    sity of Toronto Press, 1967.

Thoreau, Henry David. *The Writings of Henry David Thoreau.* Boston: Houghton Mifflin, 1892.

Thurman, Kelly. "Margaret Fuller in Two American Novels: *The Blithedale Romance and Elsie Venner.*" Master's thesis, University of Kentucky, 1945.

Urbanski, Marie Olesen. "The Ambivalence of Ralph Waldo Emerson towards Margaret Fuller." *Thoreau Journal Quarterly* 10 (July 1978): 26–36.

————. "Henry David Thoreau and Margaret Fuller." *Thoreau Journal Quarterly* 8 (October 1976): 24–30.

Violette, Augusta Genevieve. *Economic Feminism in American Literature Prior to 1848.* Orono, Maine: University Press, 1925.

Wade, Mason. *Margaret Fuller: Whetstone of Genius.* New York: Viking Press, 1940.

Wardle, Ralph M. *Mary Wollstonecraft: A Critical Biography.* Lawrence: University of Kansas Press, 1951.

Waterman, William Randall. *Frances Wright.* 1924. Rpt., New York: AMS Press, 1967.

Webb, Robert Kiefer. *Harriet Martineau, A Radical Victorian.* London: Heinemann, 1960.

Welter, Barbara. *Dimity Convictions: The American Woman in the Nineteenth Century.* Athens: Ohio University Press, 1976.

Wheatley, Vera. *The Life and Work of Harriet Martineau.* London: Secker & Warburg, 1957.

Whicher, George F. *The Transcendentalist Revolt against Materialism.* Boston: D. C. Heath, 1949.

Wollstonecraft, Mary. *A Vindication of the Rights of Woman.* Edited by Charles W. Hagelman, Jr. 1792. Rpt., New York: W. W. Norton, 1967.

Wright, Frances. *Views of Society and Manners in America.* Edited by Paul R. Baker. 1821. Rpt., Cambridge: Harvard University Press, 1963.

# Index

symbolized by sea-captain image, 138, 161-62, 164, 170; as feminist manifesto, 33, 39-40, 169; publishing history of: 163, 167-68, 171; reviews of: *Boston Courier,* 147; *Broadway Journal,* 148-49; *Brownson's Quarterly Review,* 128, 149-50; *Christian Examiner,* 150; *Christian Herald,* 167; *Godey's Magazine and Lady's* *Book,* 150; *Ladies' National Magazine,* 150; *London Quarterly Review,* 153; *New York Evening Post,* 148; *New York Tribune,* 147; *Southern Quarterly Review,* 151-52; *Spectator,* 157-58

Wright, (Fanny) Frances, (Madame D'Arusmont), 62-65, 67 n.26, 88, 99, 116, 124, 164

Wright, Martha C., 158

## ABOUT THE AUTHOR

MARIE MITCHELL OLESEN URBANSKI is Associate Professor of English at the University of Maine in Orono and editor of *Thoreau Journal Quarterly*. Her essays will appear in *Critical Essays on Margaret Fuller* ( Joel Myerson, ed.), and in *Publishers for Mass Entertainment in the 19th Century* (Madeleine B. Stern, ed.). She has contributed articles to *Thoreau Journal Quarterly*, *Studies in Short Fiction*, and *Harvard Magazine*.